The Radical Act of Saving Your Damn Self!

Breaking free from people-pleasing, perfectionism and self-betrayal

by

Kiana Jordan

This publication, in part or whole, may not be reproduced, stored or transmitted in any form—electronic, mechanical, recording or otherwise—without prior written consent from the author.

All rights reserved.

Copyright © Connection Centered Coaching 2025

ISBN: 979-8-9929172-0-8

Published By: Kiana Jordan

Website: www.kianajordan.com

Table Of Contents

Chapter One: The Radical Act of Saving Your Damn Self 1

Chapter Two: Curiosity: Awareness Without Judgment 3

Chapter Three: Clarity: Seeing Yourself in the Big Picture 18

Chapter Four: Courage: It's Time to Face Yourself 32

Chapter Five: Compassion: Beyond Judgment: Choosing Compassion Over 51

Chapter Six: Care: Treating Yourself Like the Treasure You Are 67

Chapter Seven: Consistency: Building the Foundation for Lasting Change 85

Chapter Eight: Your INNEREVOLUTION in Real Life: Stories, Shifts, and the Space to Begin 100

Chapter Nine: Conclusion: The Beginning of Your
Radical Journey 121

Epilogue 126

Acknowledgements 127

Dedication

For every daughter, niece, and granddaughter…

For the girls who will grow into women, the women who are still healing the girls they once were, and the generations who deserve to inherit something greater than survival.

May you always know your worth is **NOT** negotiable. Your voice is **NOT** optional. Your presence **IS** a gift.

And may this book be the last time you need to be told.

Foreword

I won't waste your time by telling you this book will change your life—because you already know that's not how transformation works.

Books don't change lives. Decisions do.

If you're holding this book in your hands, cracked it open and made it this far, you've already made one: <u>The decision to stop living in survival mode and start building a life that actually honors you.</u>

I don't know what brought you here. Maybe you're exhausted from constantly being everything to everyone. Maybe you've spent years shrinking yourself to fit into spaces that were never meant for you.

Maybe you've read every self-help book, taken every class, followed every guru, and still feel like you're running in circles—still stuck, waiting, wondering when your turn will come.

Or maybe you've finally realized something so many of us take so long to understand:

No one is coming to save you.

The person you're waiting for...The version of you that feels grounded, confident, fully in her power. She isn't going to appear out of thin air. She isn't waiting on a better job, the right relationship, more money, or the perfect moment.

She is waiting on you.

To decide. To commit. To stop making excuses and start making changes.

To stop prioritizing everyone else's expectations and start prioritizing yourself.

That's what makes this book is different. It's not a passive, feel-good read that will collect dust on your shelf while you wait for a spark of motivation. This is an invitation. A call-in. A moment to get real with yourself about who you are, what you need, and what you are no longer willing to tolerate.

Inside these pages, you will be introduced to The **C6 Blueprint™: Curiosity, Clarity, Courage, Compassion, Care, and Consistency.** This isn't just a framework—it's a way of being. It's a foundation that will help you break free from old patterns, build self-trust, and stop performing a life that doesn't fit you and your values and goals.

It will push you. It will challenge you.

And if you let it, *it will transform you.*

But let me be clear: Nothing in this book will work unless you do.

Reading won't save you.

Knowing better won't change you. Only doing better will.

So let this be the last time you start something that you don't finish it. The last time you collect wisdom without applying it. The last time you let fear, doubt, or perfectionism keep you from your own damn evolution.

Because the life you want. The one where you don't have to explain yourself, shrink yourself, or betray yourself just to keep the peace. It's already yours.

Now claim it.

Introduction: This Isn't a Self-Help Book. It's a Self-Return Manual.

I want to be clear from the start—this isn't a self-help book and I'm not here to coddle you. If you're looking for quick fixes or glittery affirmations, this isn't that kind of ride. But if you know the exhaustion of always striving to be "good enough," when you don't even know who you're trying to prove it to—keep reading.

I know what it feels like to move through life like you're on autopilot—pushing, performing, people-pleasing—until one day, you look up and realize you've built a life that doesn't even belong to you.

This book won't tell you to "just think positive" or "trust the process." It won't ask you to bypass your pain or slap a smile on top of your burnout. You won't find empty affirmations or sugarcoated advice within these pages.

You'll find truth. Reflection. Tools. And maybe, if you're ready—a path back to yourself.

You don't need another plan to become "better." You need a system to remember who you are beneath the mask—and *permission* to stay there.

Because here's the truth: Transformation isn't easy, and **no one is coming to save you.**

For far too long, you've been waiting. Waiting for clarity. Waiting for confidence. Waiting for someone to give you permission to take up space.

But what if I told you that moment isn't coming? That the version of you who is strong, decisive, and deeply powerful isn't waiting for better circumstances—she's waiting for you to start showing up.

The Art of Saving Your Damn Self is about the radical act of deciding, once and for all, that you are done betraying yourself. That you will no longer put yourself last. You are ready to step into who you are meant to be.

Because make no mistake—saving yourself is radical. In a world that teaches women to be agreeable, accommodating, self-sacrificing, and endlessly nurturing to everyone while neglecting themselves. Choosing yourself is an act of rebellion.

And I want you to get $REAL$ comfortable with rebellion.

Why This Book Exists

I know what it's like to feel invisible in a room full of people. To be the one everyone leans on, while secretly wondering who *you* can lean on. To feel like you've checked all the right boxes—kind, responsible, successful, generous—only to feel *empty*.

I know the exhaustion of always striving to be "good enough," when you don't even know who you're trying to prove it to. The drowning in expectations that were never yours to carry in the first place.

For over a decade, I thought I was doing everything right. I said yes when I wanted to say no. I prioritized being likable over being honest. I avoided conflict, even when it meant betraying my own needs and feelings. I convinced myself that if I worked harder—at my job, my relationships, my life—then one day, I'd feel whole.

But that day never came.

Instead, I woke up one morning and realized something that changed everything: I wasn't waiting for my life to get better. I was waiting for permission to live it.

That's when I realized I had two choices: Keep waiting, hoping that someday I'd magically become the version of me I was meant to be…or I could decide that someday is today. This book is about helping you make that same decision.

A Framework for Saving Yourself

Transformation doesn't happen on accident. It's not something you stumble into. It's something you build, one decision at a time.

Introduction: This Isn't a Self-Help Book. It's a Self-Return Manual.

The Radical Act of Saving Your Damn Self! isn't a step-by-step manual for perfection...

...It's broken into chapters based on the C6 Blueprint™ I created through my own INNEREVOLUTION™.

These six pillars are the foundation of self-trust, self-respect, and radical self-ownership:

- **Curiosity** helps you question the narratives that have kept you stuck.
- **Clarity** gives you the power to define your own damn life.
- **Courage** pushes you to take action, even when you're scared.
- **Compassion** teaches you to extend grace to yourself, instead of tearing yourself down.
- **Care** reminds you that your well-being is nonnegotiable.
- **Consistency** ensures that all of this isn't just a temporary shift—it becomes who you are.

This isn't a feel-good framework. It's not about surface-level inspiration. It's about creating real, lasting change that doesn't disappear the moment life gets hard.

What You Won't Find in This Book

I'm not here to sell you toxic positivity or make you feel like you need to earn your worth through endless self-improvement.

I won't tell you to "just be grateful" when you're struggling. I won't pretend healing is a linear, picture-perfect journey. And I sure as hell won't be suggesting that self-care is as simple as taking bubble baths and drinking more water.

Instead, I'm going to challenge you. I'm going to push you to ask yourself hard questions. I'm going to hold up a mirror and ask you if you like the person staring back at you—not because you need fixing, but because you deserve to see yourself clearly.

The Art of Saving Your Damn Self is about waking up.

It's about stepping into the version of you that no longer tolerates half-lived dreams, watered-down truths, or people who only love you when it's convenient.

It's about making **bold, unapologetic choices** that honor the woman you are becoming.

Who This Book Is For

If you've ever felt like you were too much or not enough at the same time, this book is for you. If you've ever felt like you've given every version of yourself away to others and have nothing left for yourself, keep reading. If you're tired of waiting for your life to start, tired of shrinking, tired of being stuck in the cycle of *almost*, this book is for you.

But this book is not for everyone.

If you want easy answers, quick fixes, or a magic formula to make your life perfect overnight, this is not the book for you.

If you are comfortable blaming everyone else for where you are and aren't willing to look inward, this is not the book for you.

This book is for the woman who is ready. Ready to take up space. Ready to stop apologizing for existing. Ready to take radical responsibility for her own damn life.

How to Use This Book

Read it in pieces.

Quiet or loudly contemplate.

Take it slow or binge it all in one sitting.

Write in the margins. Cry. Laugh. Cuss if you need to.

But more than anything—**tell the truth to yourself.**

Because the moment you do that, the saving has already started.

Your Journey Starts Here

This book won't save you. But you will.

You'll save yourself every time you choose honesty over avoidance. Every time you enforce a boundary instead of bending to make others comfortable. Every time you show up for yourself, even when no one else is watching.

This is your invitation.

To wake up.

To take up space.

To rewrite every rule that has kept you small.

The only question left is: *Are you ready?*

Let's begin.

Chapter One

The Radical Act of Saving Your Damn Self

You don't save yourself all at once.

You do it in small moments—when you tell the truth even though your voice shakes, when you say no without guilt, when you stop abandoning yourself to keep the peace.

Saving yourself isn't glamorous. It's gritty. It's honest. And most of all—it's yours.

I used to think saving myself meant hustling harder. That if I could just get the right title, the right body, the right relationship—then I'd finally feel whole. But the truth? I was collecting achievements while bleeding out emotionally. I wasn't living. I was performing.

The moment that changed everything wasn't loud or dramatic. It was quiet. It was me, sitting in my car, realizing that I didn't recognize the woman I had become. I was exhausted, resentful, disconnected—and terrified to admit that I had built a life that looked good from the outside but was crushing me from the inside.

That was my wake-up call.

That was the moment I stopped waiting to be rescued. That was the day I chose me.

What Does It Mean to Save Yourself?

It means you stop outsourcing your worth.

It means you stop waiting for permission.

It means you remember you were never broken to begin with.

The radical act of saving your damn self is not about becoming someone new—it's about **returning to who you were before the world told you who to be.** It's about reclaiming your power, your presence, your peace.

It's not easy. But it's worth it. And you don't have to do it perfectly—you just have to start.

Chapter Two

Curiosity: Awareness Without Judgment

Curiosity doesn't just open doors—it blows the damn walls down. It's the mindset that takes you from spiraling in self-doubt to standing in self-awareness. When you stop asking, "What's wrong with me?" and start asking, "What's really going on here?" you're giving yourself permission to see the truth without judgment. Curiosity isn't about tearing yourself apart; it's about understanding what's happening beneath the surface so you can grow from it.

At its core, curiosity is quiet courage. It takes guts to look at the messy, unpolished parts of yourself without shame or excuses. But that's where the magic lies. You don't need to like everything you find—this isn't about sugarcoating. It's about being honest with yourself and holding space for what's real. Curiosity isn't here to beat you up; it's here to help you see clearly.

When you start asking the right questions, everything changes. You stop being a passenger in your own life and take the damn wheel. Stop living on autopilot, repeating old patterns, and start making choices that actually serve you. Curiosity doesn't just create clarity—it creates freedom. When you see things as they are, you can finally decide what comes next. This is where your power lies.

***

For most of my life, I would hear the same thing: *"You're too nice."* My go-to response*: "I'm not too nice—I'm kind."* I said it with confidence, convinced that my ability to avoid conflict and keep the peace made me a *good* person. But the hard truth is: I was lying.

I wasn't kind. I was scared. And I didn't have the curiosity to ask myself why.

When I realized this, it felt like mourning a version of myself I had carefully crafted and protected for decades. I sat with the uncomfortable truth that I wasn't being kind; I was avoiding. I wasn't choosing peace—I was choosing silence. I wasn't making conscious decisions. I was reacting, shrinking, and hoping that by keeping my head down I could avoid the discomfort of being misunderstood, judged, or rejected.

But avoidance has its own consequences.

One particular moment cracked this wide open for me. I was driving for Uber when a differently-abled man wheeled up to my car, soaking wet. The smell hit me immediately, and my first instinct was to ask him to change into dry clothes before getting in. But instead of speaking up, I swallowed my discomfort and stayed silent.

The whole ride, I was furious. Not at him. At myself.

Why hadn't I said something? Why had I abandoned my own needs in that moment? The answer hit me harder than I care to admit: I didn't want to seem rude. I didn't want to be perceived as mean. My fear of being disliked, of being seen as insensitive, overpowered my ability to act honestly. And be true to myself.

Later, I told my partner about the experience. When they said, *"You're too nice,"* I snapped: *"I'm not nice! You wouldn't say that if you knew the thoughts in my head."*

But deep down, I knew the truth. I wasn't being kind. I was avoiding discomfort. I was avoiding the possibility of being seen as anything less than *perfect*.

The Pattern of Avoidance

When I failed my Physical Training (PT) test, the fallout felt like the final straw. My promotion was on hold, and I stood in front of my Group Commander, facing a written reprimand. I was drowning in shame and exhaustion, but instead of asking myself why I was struggling, I did what I had always done: I avoided the hard questions.

I wasn't curious about why I was stuck. Or how I was feeling or why I was so burned out. I was working out, sure—but I wasn't addressing the deeper issues. My stress. My fear. My emotional depletion.

As a single mom juggling two $0 paychecks and leading a brand-new team, I convinced myself that holding it together on the outside was enough. That if I just keep pushing, if I keep showing up, I could avoid looking at what was bubbling beneath the surface.

But avoidance is a trap. And the truth will always demand to be seen.

I told myself I was choosing peace—but really, I was using it as a shield to avoid accountability. Once I started paying attention, I saw this pattern everywhere in my life.

The Wake-Up Call

What I didn't realize at the time was that curiosity could've saved me. If I had asked myself even one question—*Why do I feel like this?*—I may have seen the truth sooner.

I wasn't operating from kindness, strength, or peace. I was running on empty. I was clinging to an identity that no longer served me, afraid to admit that I had outgrown the person I once was.

And the moment that woke me up. It wasn't a big, dramatic revelation. It was the quiet realization that I wasn't even in my own story anymore.

I had written myself out of my own life, convinced that my

worth was tied to how others saw me. I let their approval—or the fear of their disapproval—shape my every move.

And when I finally got curious, everything changed.

The Power of Asking Better Questions

Stop and ask yourself:

- Why am I afraid to speak up?
- What am I really avoiding?
- Who am I trying to protect?
- What do I actually want?

These questions are uncomfortable—messy, even—but they crack open the truth.

I realized that my so-called peace was fear in disguise. I wasn't keeping the peace,

I was keeping myself small.

Curiosity teaches you to sit with the discomfort instead of running from it. It shows that asking the right questions doesn't make you weak—it makes you free. You aren't protecting anyone by staying silent, and definitely not protecting yourself. Don't get stuck in a cycle of fear, avoidance, and people-pleasing curiosity is the only way out.

Curiosity is the First Step Back to Yourself

Looking back now, I see that version of me—the one who stayed quiet and called it kindness—with compassion. She wasn't weak. She wasn't broken. She was scared.

But here's what I now know: *Fear is an invitation to become curious.*

Curiosity is what helps you stop hiding. It's what helps you see yourself clearly—messy parts and all—and still move forward.

I stopped asking, *"What's wrong with me?"* and started asking, *"What's really going on with me?"*

That one mindset shift pulled me out of survival mode and back into own my story. I learned that I didn't have to prove my worth through over-giving. I didn't have to silence myself to avoid discomfort. I didn't have to pretend I was fine when I wasn't.

I just had to be willing to ask the right questions and face the answers.

The Question That Changes Everything

I'm not too nice.

I'm not a coward.

I'm not small.

I am someone who learned to get curious—and that curiosity brought me back to myself. And now, I want to ask you the questions that changed everything for me:

- What are you avoiding?
- What truth is waiting for you beneath your fear?
- What would happen if you got curious?

Because once you do, once you start asking the questions that matter, you'll realize something that will change your life:

You were never too much.
You were never not enough.
You were never meant to live in fear.

It's time to get curious. It's time to come back home to yourself.

Curiosity is about asking the real questions—the ones that make you pause, reflect, and get honest with yourself. It's not about judgment or tearing yourself apart. It's about looking at your choices, patterns, and beliefs with fresh eyes and an open heart.

Take a moment to sit with these questions:

- **When was the last time you said yes when you really wanted to say no?** What was going through your mind? Were you trying to avoid conflict, keep the peace, or stay in someone's good graces? How did it feel afterward? What did it cost you?
- **What story are you telling yourself about what it means to be kind?** Does kindness mean keeping quiet, shrinking yourself, or prioritizing others no matter what? Where did this idea come from? Is it actually serving you—or holding you back?
- **What are you pretending not to know about yourself?** What truths have you been pushing aside because they feel too messy, scary, or uncomfortable to face?
- **What would change if you prioritized curiosity over criticism?** Instead of asking, 'What's wrong with me?' try this: 'What's really happening beneath the surface? How would that shift how you treat yourself?

Let these questions guide you The answers might surprise you, and that's where the real growth begins.

Curiosity starts with slowing down and getting real about what's actually happening—not just surface-level emotions, but deeper fears and patterns driving your thoughts and reactions. It's about stepping back, asking questions, and making space for understanding instead of spiraling into judgment or blame.

Ready to practice curiosity on purpose? Start here.

- **Name the Fear**

  Get brutally honest about what's holding you back. Is it the fear of rejection? Being disliked? Avoiding conflict? Not living up to expectations? Call it what it is. Naming the fear doesn't make it disappear, but it strips its control over you. Instead of operating from a place of avoidance, empower yourself to acknowledge and face it.

- **Challenge the Narrative**

  Ask yourself: "Is this fear even real, or am I just running on an old story I've outgrown?" So often, our deepest fears are rooted in outdated beliefs—things we learned in our childhood, past relationships, or moments of failure that no longer apply. Be curious about where those stories came from and whether they still hold today.

- **Shift to Curiosity Instead of Judgment**

  When something triggers you, instead of shutting down or blaming yourself or others, stop and ask:

"Why am I feeling this way? What's really going on here?" This isn't about excusing bad behavior or avoiding accountability—it's about understanding yourself on a deeper level so you can respond thoughtfully instead of reacting impulsively.

Curiosity is a muscle you build one moment at a time. Each time you choose to ask questions instead of making assumptions, you strengthen your relationship with yourself. Your fears and triggers aren't enemies—they're invitations to look deeper.

The next time you feel stuck, overwhelmed, or reactive, stop. Get curious. What you learn in that moment could change everything.

Curiosity means more than looking inward. It's noticing when you're overwhelmed, when your yes isn't honest, and getting honest about what's driving it. One of the most powerful ways to practice curiosity in real time is by setting boundaries, starting with a simple but challenging step: Saying no without over-explaining.

The next time someone asks for your time, energy, or help and it doesn't align with what you can give, try this: *"I can't help you today, but I hope things work out."*

That's it. No long-winded excuse, no guilt-filled backtracking—just a clear, kind no. Then, pause. Notice what happens in your body. Does it feel uncomfortable?

Empowering? Both? Pay attention to how it feels to honor your boundaries instead of trying to justify them. Let yourself sit with that feeling without judgment. Then, get curious:

- What made saying "no" hard (if it was)?
- How did it feel to honor what you needed?
- What story have you been telling yourself about why you "can't" say "no?"

This isn't about getting it perfect. It's about practicing curiosity in the moments that matter most.

Every time you take a step like this, you're proving to yourself that your boundaries matter. That your needs are just as important as anyone else's. It won't always feel easy—but it will always be worth it. Keep practicing. You've got this.

***

Curiosity is the foundation of self-awareness—not self-criticism. Every time you ask yourself an honest question *without judgment,* you start rewriting the story that deems you powerless. The truth. You've always had a choice—you're just now waking up to it.

When you lean into curiosity, you start seeing things for what they really are. It's not about being perfect. It's not about having it all figured out. It's about pausing long enough to ask yourself, *"What's really going on here?"* This one question can shift everything. It pulls you out of autopilot and into awareness.

Take a look at the moments you stayed quiet, the times you said yes when you really wanted to say no, and the patterns you've been stuck in—not to blame yourself, but to understand. Because when you get to the root of why you've been stuck, you give yourself the power to make a new choice. **These moments usually aren't random—they're rooted in something deeper.**

When you pause to notice what's underneath, you can start naming the stories that shaped your responses.

- Maybe you said yes out of fear of disappointing someone.
- Maybe you avoided confrontation because conflict feels unsafe.
- Maybe you keep yourself small because you were taught that being "too much" would push people away.

Whatever the reason, **curiosity gives you the space to name it, face it, and rewrite it.**

Every time you choose curiosity over criticism, you're building something new. Remind yourself that your story isn't set in stone. You are not trapped in old patterns—you're simply in the process of unlearning them.

Keep asking the hard questions. Keep showing up for yourself. Keep choosing understanding over shame.

This is how change begins.

It's curiosity that turns autopilot off and brings you back to presence. It's not about finding quick fixes, rushing to solutions, or beating yourself up for where you are. It's about slowing down and asking the right questions.

Looking back, you've explored how curiosity helps you uncover what's driving your choices and patterns. It's about noticing your fears, reactions, and the stories you've been telling yourself—not criticize, but learn. Because the truth is, **awareness is the first step to change.** You can't shift what you refuse to see, and curiosity is a tool that helps you see clearly.

But curiosity isn't just about looking inward. It's also about how you approach the world around you. When you stay open, ask better questions, and release assumptions, you create space for stronger connections, healthier boundaries, and more intentional decisions. You stop reacting out of habit and start **deciding** with clarity.

Curiosity doesn't demand perfection—it invites honesty. It doesn't rush you into change, but it nudges you forward.

It asks, *"What's here that I haven't noticed before?"* and *"What's possible if I allow myself to see things differently?"*

And this is where courage comes in.

Because curiosity shows you what needs to change, courage is what helps you take the leap. It's one thing to recognize your patterns—it's another to do something about them.

In the next chapter, we'll explore what it means to step into courage—to act on what you now understand, to stand in your truth, and to break free from what no longer serves you.

Curiosity wakes you up. Courage moves you forward.

Take the next step.

Notes

These pages are for you—your reflections, breakthroughs, questions, and reminders.
Write what you need to say. Cross it out. Rewrite it.
This is your space to be messy, honest, and free.

Chapter Three

Clarity: Seeing Yourself in the Big Picture

Clarity is the practice of reducing ambiguity about yourself by understanding and embracing that your core values, beliefs, vision, priorities, and goals do not require anyone else's validation. They stand firm because they are yours.

While I was in the military, clarity was built into everything we did. The organization has a mission, vision, goals, and priorities that ensures everyone is aligned. We knew where we were going, how we fit into the bigger picture, and why our contributions mattered. That kind of clarity made it easy to feel purpose-driven and disciplined. And let's be real—it felt good to be recognized for your contributions, have people rally behind you, and know that success wasn't just about you. A win for one was a win for all.

But here's the problem: When you step out of that structured environment that clarity doesn't follow you. If you haven't defined your own mission, vision, goals, and priorities, it's easy to get lost. Instead of being anchored in who you are, you start leaning on external expectations to tell you what to do, who to be, and where to go.

Clarity isn't just about having a plan or a goal—it's about believing who you are. It's about standing firm in your truth, no matter who's watching, no matter who's clapping.

***

I've always loved bringing people together—to learn, celebrate, motivate, empower, and connect. Whether it's gathering for deep conversations or simply sharing a laugh over life's ups and downs, connection has always been at the core of who I am. Nurturing relationships has always been one of my highest values. I've never been the type to live by, "No new friends." I've always welcomed people in with an open heart.

But even with a love for connection, you have to have a firm line: no disloyalty, no mean-spiritedness, and no envy. Those values have been my nonnegotiables. But having values isn't enough if you're not clear about them with people around you.

One day, a group I was part of came crashing down because of a massive miscommunication. I trusted someone to speak on my behalf, assuming they'd be careful and accurate, that they'd honor our alignment. Instead, I was betrayed. What hurt even more was that others believed the lies spread about me—despite my actions always aligning with my words. I felt violated, exposed, and humiliated. My response? I took my proverbial ball and went home.

That decision shocked people, but it didn't surprise me. I saw the cracks forming for a while. I was hurt and resentful, but looking back, I see where I went wrong. I wasn't clear about my boundaries. Instead of addressing the issues head-on, I stayed silent—until I couldn't anymore. And instead of having the hard conversations, I walked away.

Another instance was when I was being slandered online. My subordinates whispered about me, and my leaders believed the rumors without ever having a conversation with me. It was devastating. But instead of standing up for myself, I withdrew. I didn't quit my job, but I emotionally shut down. I distanced myself from everyone.

My work ethic didn't change—I showed up and did everything that was expected of me. But inside, I was fuming. I was heartbroken that people I trusted could believe lies about me instead of simply asking me what was true. That betrayal burned me so badly I reached out to a mentor and secured an assignment transfer as fast as I could.

Sometimes silence can feel like power. Like walking away and keeping your distance can protect you from further hurt. But all it does was make you feel more isolated and more resentful. You will spend countless hours replaying the same situation in your head, asking yourself: *Why didn't they just talk to me? And why didn't I say something first?*

Silent treatment and distance never sat well with me, so being unfriended by people I considered close friends was a pain I wasn't prepared for. It happened twice over the years, and both times, it stung deeply. I spent so much time mourning those friendships and replaying every interaction, wondering if I was to blame. I kept asking myself: *"What did I do wrong?" "How could I have done better?"*

It wasn't until my late 30s that I realized the real problem: I wasn't clear. A lack of standards and clarity in my relationships can cause more pain than necessary. I wasn't being upfront about my expectations, my boundaries, or what I needed to feel respected. I assumed people knew what I stood for, but I never actually said it out loud.

I was working under a supervisor I deeply respected. I believed this person had my best interests at heart. Until one day, I asked for clarification on an issue, and their response shocked me. My question was interpreted as insubordination. What followed was a humiliating meeting with multiple leaders where I was verbally bashed for simply seeking understanding.

That experience left me feeling betrayed—not just by my supervisor, but by the entire organization I had dedicated so much of my life to. It was one of the defining moments that led to my decision to retire.

Looking back, I see the common thread in all these experiences was a lack of clarity—both on my part and on theirs. I hadn't taken the time to name my expectations, express my boundaries, or articulate what I truly needed from the people around me. I expected people would just know, but expectations leave room for misunderstanding and resentment.

Clarity isn't just about knowing your values—it is about communicating your values, standing firm in them, and creating space for others to honor them too. It's about reducing ambiguity in your relationships, your decisions, and how you show up in the world.

This lesson didn't come easy, but it taught me something I'll carry with me forever: <u>Clarity is the foundation for connection, respect, and alignment</u>. Without it, you drift through life, letting others define your worth. With it, you anchor yourself in your truth and create the life and relationships you truly deserve.

When You Don't Say It, They Can't See It

Clarity is not just about knowing your values—it's about communicating them. Without clarity, the strongest relationships can crumble.

For so long, I avoided the hard conversations. I told myself it wasn't worth it—that I was too much, too sensitive, or just too difficult to understand.

Maybe you've done that too. Maybe you've convinced yourself that being misunderstood is just part of who you are. That people won't "get" you no matter how hard you try.

But here's the truth I couldn't see at the time: They didn't know who I was because I never gave them the chance to.

I assumed that if people really cared, they would just know what I needed. That they would pick up on my discomfort, my boundaries, my values, my unspoken expectations.

But how could they?

When you spend so much time trying to be agreeable, easygoing, and "not a burden," you end up hiding your real self—not just from others, but from yourself. If you've ever felt this way—frustrated, unseen, or like no one fully understands you— it's time to ask some hard questions. Because if you don't understand yourself, how can you expect others to?

Here are a few questions to help you start seeing yourself clearly:

- What core values guide me, even when no one is watching?
- What would I pursue if fear of judgment or failure wasn't in the way?
- Whose approval am I still chasing, and why?
- What truly matters to me beyond recognition or external reward?

These aren't easy questions, but they *will* change everything. Because when you know who you are, you stop assuming, shrinking, or waiting for people to see you. You show up with clarity. No more second-guessing, no more assumptions—just the truth of who you are.

And that truth? It's worth standing in.

Clarity isn't just about knowing what you believe—it's about **living it**. It's the foundation for how you make decisions, set boundaries, and navigate the world with confidence. Without clarity, it's easy to drift, reacting to life instead of leading it. But when you take time to understand what truly matters to you, every choice becomes more intentional. You can start practicing clarity by:

- **Own Your Core Values**

    Your values are the nonnegotiables that guide you, even when no one is watching.

    Identifying them is the first step toward clarity. Take time to write down values that matter most to you—such as like honesty, freedom, integrity, growth, or respect. Then ask yourself:

    o   *Why do these values matter to me?*

    o   *How do they show up in my daily life?*

    o   *What happens when I ignore or compromise them?*

    For example, if honesty is a core value, notice

how it influences your relationships and decision-making. Owning your values means ensuring your actions consistently reflect them.

- **Create A Personal Vision**

    Clarity is knowing what kind of life you're building. Your personal vision isn't about rigid goals—it's about defining the bigger picture of what matters to you. Ask yourself:

    - *What do I want my life to stand for?*
    - *How do I want to feel in my career, relationships, and daily life?*
    - *What kind of impact do I want to have?*

    Writing down a clear, personal vision statement helps you make decisions that align with your long-term growth. It's your **North Star**, keeping you grounded even when things feel uneasy.

- **Check for Alignment**

    Every decision you make either supports or detracts from your clarity. The next time you're faced with a choice, pause and ask:

    - *Does this align with my values and vision?*

> o   *Am I making this decision out of fear, habit, or pressure from others?*

If something doesn't align, take a step back. The more you practice, the easier it becomes to make choices that reflects who you truly are.

- **Filter Out the Noise**

    Not all advice, expectations, or opinions are worth your energy. Clarity helps you know what to keep and what to release. The next time someone gives you feedback, ask yourself:

    > o   *Is this helping me grow, or is it rooted in my fears or expectations?*

    > o   *Does this resonate with my values, or am I just trying to please others?*

    When you stop letting outside noise dictate your path, you will reclaim your power.

Clarity is a Daily Practice

Clarity isn't something you achieve once—it's something you commit to daily. By owning your values, defining your vision, and making aligned choices, you create a life that reflects who you are—not who the world expects you to be.

Without a clear sense of direction, it's easy to get pulled into decisions, commitments, and expectations that don't align with who you really are. Clarity starts with defining what truly matters to you and using it as your guide. But when you take the time to identify your mission, you give yourself an anchor—something solid to hold onto when life feels messy or outside pressures threaten to pull you off course.

Take the first step by creating or refining your personal mission statement. This is your foundation. A guiding force for the life you are building.

A Simple Framework to Get Started

Try filling in the blanks:

"My life's mission is to [insert your vision] while staying aligned with [your core values]."

Here are a couple of examples:

- *"My life's mission is to [create spaces where connection and growth thrive] while staying aligned with [authenticity, curiosity, and courage]."*

- *"My life's mission is to [build a life that inspires others] while staying true to my values of [compassion, integrity, and strength]."*

Once you've written your mission, take it a step further. Reflect on one recent decision you made.

- *Did this decision align with my vision and values?*
- *Or did I let fear, habit, or someone else's expectations influenced me?*

Be honest with yourself. If the decision wasn't aligned, don't judge yourself—use it as an opportunity to learn and adjust.

Your mission statement isn't just a nice idea to write down and forget. It's a tool to help you live with intention. The more you refer back to it, the easier it becomes to make choices that feel true to you. This isn't about being perfect. It's about showing up for yourself, one intentional choice at a time.

Clarity allows you to step fully into your life as the main character—not a supporting role, not the afterthought, not the person waiting for permission. It reminds you that you don't need validation to move forward. Your values, your vision, and your goals are *enough*.

Every time you choose alignment over avoidance you're making a bold declaration:

"I am enough just as I am, and I trust myself to decide what's right for me."

Clarity gives you the strength to stop living for other people's expectations and start living for yourself. It helps you recognize when you're acting out of fear or habit instead of truth. It gives you the courage to say no to what doesn't serve you, yes to what does, and to stand in your decisions without apology.

But let's be clear—this isn't about having everything figured out. It's not about never feeling uncertain or always knowing the right move. Clarity isn't perfection. It's the willingness to pause, reflect, and make choices that feel true to who you are. It's deciding to honor your values, even when it's uncomfortable or when others don't understand.

Every step you take in alignment with your truth is a step toward the life you've always deserved. Even the small decisions—the ones no one else sees—are proof that you're choosing yourself in ways that matter.

Keep trusting yourself. Keep making choices that reflect your values. Keep stepping into who you are without hesitation.

Clarity isn't something you have to earn—it's something you already hold within you. All you have to do is claim it.

Clarity means knowing your truth—without waiting for approval, validation, or permission from anyone else. It's about defining your core values, goals, and priorities—not borrowing someone else's version of what your life should look like. When you're clear about who you are and what you want, you stop living on autopilot. You stop bending to expectations that don't align with your vision.

You step into your life with intention.

When life gets noisy, messy, or uncertain, having a clear foundation gives you something solid to stand on. It keeps you grounded in your truth, even when outside pressures try to shake you. It's not about having all the answers—it's about having an anchor that keeps you steady.

When you are clear about your mission and vision, decisions become easier. You have a filter: Does this align with who I am and what I want? Clarity helps you say "yes" to what truly matters and "no" to what doesn't—without guilt. It frees you from being pulled in a million directions so you can create a life that actually feels like yours.

Stepping into Courage

As we move into Chapter 4, remember that **clarity fuels courage**. When you know your values and vision, standing firm in your truth becomes easier—even when fear or doubt creeps in.

Clarity makes it possible to speak up, take action, and honor yourself in ways you never have before. Courage builds on clarity, turning what you know about yourself into the bold steps that create the life you deserve.

Now that you know your truth, it's time to act on it.

Let's move forward.

Notes

These pages are for you—your reflections, breakthroughs, questions, and reminders.
Write what you need to say. Cross it out. Rewrite it.
This is your space to be messy, honest, and free.

_____

_____

_____

_____

_____

_____

_____

_____

_____

_____

_____

_____

_____

_____

_____

_____

_____

_____

Chapter Four

Courage: It's Time to Face Yourself

When you have seen your life through the lens of clarity, you must then gain the courage to act. To choose yourself over others. Courage isn't just about grand acts of bravery—it's about the relentless pursuit of speaking up, standing firm, and refusing to shrink in the face of anything that contradicts your beliefs, values, and worldview. It's about advocating for yourself and others, even when it's uncomfortable, unwelcome, or goes against what society expects of you.

True courage requires deep attunement to what feels right and authentic for you. It's the drop in your stomach when you know something isn't right. The rush of heat in your chest when you realize you need to say something. The mix of fear and excitement when you're standing at the edge of something bigger than you've ever dared to claim for yourself. These are signals—your body's way of demanding your attention.

Too often, we [swallow our truth](#) to avoid confrontation or discomfort. We allow dismissive, hurtful, or undermining behavior to fester, and in doing so, we lay the foundation for resentment, exhaustion, and quiet self-betrayal. Here's a truth: Avoiding conflict doesn't protect you—it erodes you. The energy you spend suppressing your voice will eventually turn inward, showing up as anxiety, frustration, or even physically.

You don't need a warning—you picked up this book because *you have already been warned.*

You've felt it. You've lived it.

Courage is about disrupting the cycle. It's about choosing to honor yourself, your voice, and your experiences as worthy of the same care and attention you so readily give to others. It's deciding that you will no longer let fear, external validation, or outdated conditioning dictate how you show up in your own life.

Again, let's be clear, courage isn't about being fearless. Fear is part of the process. Courage is about feeling the fear but choosing to act anyway. It's about stepping forward, embracing vulnerability, and speaking your truth, even if your voice shakes.

Because at the end of the day, courage is one of the major keys to unlocking the life you deserve. It's the force that will carry you from survival to self-trust, from hesitation to action, from people-pleasing to personal power.

One **BOLD** step at a time.

Sent Away, But Not Silent

When I returned from deployment, I was reassigned to a new team—and to say I was devastated would be an understatement. The assignment was nothing short of a nightmare in my eyes—monotonous, requiring little more than accurate data entry and a working knowledge of policies and procedures. Adding insult to injury, the unit had been gutted before my arrival, leaving just enough personnel to scrape by, barely maintaining quality and accuracy. Worse still, this was where leaders often sent airmen they wanted to "stash away" until retirement or punish in subtle, yet devastating ways.

Despite the conditions, I need to be clear: The leaders who came before me were doing their best. They didn't have the rank or authority to put up much of a fight against a system that saw this team as a professional dumping ground. Their hands were tied, and it was not their fault. They could only try to maintain morale and some sense of stability in an environment that was designed to wear people down.

But that didn't make it any easier to step into.

It felt like a space where ambition had long gone unrecognized—a holding cell for potential that had never been nurtured. There was no clear direction, no engaged leadership setting the tone for growth or improvement. I refused to let that be my story.

I chose to lead with integrity, focus, and the same values that always guided me. I began cleaning house, setting clear expectations, and demonstrating that I wasn't there to be a placeholder—I was there to make an impact. Slowly, my team and I grew close. What we lacked in numbers, we made up for in camaraderie and determination. With just four of us, we were able to accomplish more than the group ever had when it was filled with disengaged airmen. For the first time in a long time, I felt like I was thriving in my role as a leader.

Then came a moment that changed everything.

I agreed to bring in new members to the team—airmen who didn't have the best reputations but whom I believed deserved a second chance. The timing was critical; we were approaching our busiest season, and I was convinced we needed all the help we could get. I also trusted in my ability to meet people where they were and guide them to become better airmen without heavy-handed discipline or threats.

For a while, my approach seemed to work. But cracks began to form as competing agendas between myself and some of my direct reports surfaced. Instead of open dialogue, there was gossip and manipulation. They started secretly talking to my leader, and I soon realized I had no real support. Instead of addressing the behaviors directly, I made the decision to prioritize their needs over my own. I convinced myself that focusing solely on my subordinates would stabilize the situation, but I couldn't have been more wrong.

The Cost of Silence

That decision did not age well.

As the weeks went on, I endured countless acts of contradiction, backstabbing, and blatant disrespect. The negativity I thought I could handle began to take a toll. I stopped recognizing myself. I, again, withdrew emotionally, began gaining weight, and spiraled into a dark place I hadn't seen since my early years in the military. Suicidal thoughts crept back in—a familiar yet unwelcome visitor I thought I left behind long ago.

I spent so much time trying to keep the peace that I completely abandoned myself in the process. I thought that if I just worked harder, if I just proved myself a little more, if I just gave people enough grace, they would eventually recognize my value and respect me.

They didn't. Because I hadn't respected myself first.

Fortunately, I sought help. Therapy became a lifeline, and for nearly a year. I worked through the pain and trauma. After a year, I was forced to stop, even though I knew I wasn't entirely healed.

Then, unexpectedly, I was up for certification in a program that I believed I had been permanently disqualified from. As part of the process, my paperwork had to be reviewed by my leaders—the very people I no longer trusted. I was pulled into my superintendent's office, where I was confronted about my mental health.

"I didn't know you were suicidal," she said, her voice heavy with concern.

What happened next would shatter every illusion I had about being supported—and force me to stand fully in my truth.

"You knew," I responded, my voice steady and unwavering. "Because I told you."

For the first time, I stood firm in my truth. I recounted every moment I reached out for help, every opportunity they were given to support me but didn't. As I spoke, my superintendent began to cry, apologizing profusely. It was as though everything I had endured culminated in that moment, and I refused to back down. I didn't yell, and I didn't flinch. I stood there, grounded in the truth of my experience, and let her feel the weight of her inaction.

That conversation marked a turning point—not just in my career but in my life. For so long, I had internalized the belief that my struggles were the fault of others. But in that moment, I realized something profound:

In every interaction, I was the common denominator.

If I didn't have the courage to set boundaries and let people know when they had me completely messed up, I was complicit in their treatment of me. My silence was being mistaken for weakness, my kindness for gullibility. By not addressing the ways I was mistreated, I allowed others to continue acting as if they were superior, entitled to direct my path while disregarding my humanity.

This realization wasn't about blame—it was about accountability. It was about reclaiming the power I had unknowingly given away.

Courage: A Chance to Stand in My Truth

I came to understand that real courage isn't just about defending others—it's about showing up for yourself when it matters most. It's about recognizing your worth and demanding others do the same. It's about making the hard choice to speak, even when your voice shakes.

From that day forward, I vowed to never again let fear or discomfort silence me. Stop sitting in spaces that did not value you. I would no longer tolerate leadership that failed to lead with integrity. I would no longer put everyone else's comfort above my own well-being.

Courage became my **North Star**—the guiding principle that allowed me to rebuild, heal, and grow. It wasn't an easy journey, but it is worth every painful step.

I pass this truth on to you: You do not have to wait for permission to take up space. You do not have to endure mistreatment to prove your resilience. You do not have to keep the peace at the cost of your own well-being.

You are allowed to take up space. You are allowed to use your voice. You are allowed to demand better.

This is what courage looks like. It is the moment you decide that your truth, your needs, and your well-being are *nonnegotiable*. It is the moment you stop asking for permission and start owning your space.

The world will not always be ready for you. But that is no longer your burden to carry. Your only job is to be ready for yourself.

Facing Fear, Reclaiming Power

Courage is not the absence of fear—it's the willingness to face discomfort and act anyway. It requires standing up for yourself and others, even when it feels risky, when it challenges long-held habits of staying silent, avoiding conflict, or prioritizing others' comfort over your own truth.

Take a moment to reflect on the following:

- **Can you recall a moment when you failed to speak up for yourself or your beliefs?**
    - What stopped you? Was it fear of rejection, conflict, or being seen as "difficult?"
    - What might have changed if you had spoken up?
- **What are the physical or emotional signals your body gives when you feel fear or discomfort?**
    - Do you feel a tightness in your chest? A sinking feeling in your stomach?

- o What if, instead of seeing these sensations as signs to retreat, you recognized them as signals guiding you toward courageous action?

- **Think of a time when you witnessed or experienced an injustice but chose to remain silent.**
  - o What was the cost of that silence?
  - o Did it leave you feeling powerless, frustrated, or resentful?

- **How has fear, self-doubt, or the need to be liked impacted your willingness to set boundaries or advocate for yourself?**
  - o Have you softened your voice, allowed disrespect, or tolerated mistreatment just to keep the peace?

Write freely, without judgment. Your reflections are not about blame—they are about understanding. When you recognize the moments where fear dictated your choices, you create space for something different.

Let these insights be a guide. Where could courage create transformation in your life?

Where have you been shrinking when you were meant to stand tall?

Courage isn't just something you have—it's something you practice. It requires intentional action, especially when fear and discomfort try to convince you to stay silent, shrink, or avoid confrontation. But each time you choose courage over comfort you reinforce your ability to show up for yourself and stand in your truth.

Here are some steps to help you in putting courage into action:

1. **Listen to Your Body's Signals**

   Fear, discomfort, and even excitement often appear in your body before you fully process them mentally. Maybe it's the drop in your stomach, the tightening in your chest, or the racing of your heart. These sensations aren't signs of weakness—they're your body alerting you to something important. Instead of pushing them away, pause and listen. What are these signals telling you? Are they nudging you to speak up, step forward, or pay closer attention?

2. **Name What's Out of Alignment**

   Courage starts with awareness. If something feels off, get specific about what that might be. Is a boundary being crossed? Is an expectation placed on you that doesn't align with your values? Are you staying silent when you should be speaking up?

Write it down. Naming the issue gives you clarity and a stronger foundation to act with intention.

3. **Speak Up—Even If Your Voice Shakes**

    It's not fearlessness or volume that defines courage—it's the willingness to act with integrity, even when it's hard. It's about being truthful. Even if it feels messy, even if your voice shakes, it starts the conversation. Take action. Advocate for yourself. The more you practice expressing your perspective clearly and respectfully, the more natural it will become.

4. **Stand Firm in Your Values**

    Courage is not about winning an argument or proving a point—it's about honoring yourself. Remind yourself why this moment matters. Whether you're setting a boundary, calling out injustice, or simply refusing to stay small, your courage is rooted in your commitment to your values. Let that be your guide.

5. **Reflect and Recalibrate**

    Afterward, take time to reflect: What went well? What felt challenging? Courage is a practice, and each act of bravery, no matter how small, strengthens your ability to act with integrity in the future. If something doesn't go as planned, don't let it discourage you. Learn from it and keep moving forward.

Courage is a Daily Choice

Courage doesn't mean the fear disappears. It means you choose to act in alignment with your values despite it. The more you practice these steps in small, everyday moments, the more naturally courage will become a part of who you are.

You are stronger than your fears. Keep showing up. Keep standing in your truth.

You've got this.

Courage doesn't happen in grand, sweeping gestures—it starts with one small, intentional act. A single decision to stop staying silent, to stop pushing your needs aside just because it feels easier or safer. You've likely had moments where you felt dismissed, overlooked, or where someone crossed a boundary and you let it slide.

Ready to take your first real step toward courage? Here's how:

- **Get Clear on the Issue**

    Think of one moment that still doesn't sit right with you. Maybe someone disregarded your feelings, crossed a boundary, or treated you in a way that felt off. Write down exactly what happened and why it bothered you. This isn't about dwelling on the past—it's about naming what's been weighing on you so you can stop carrying it alone. Getting clear gives your feelings somewhere to land—and your healing somewhere to begin.

- **Honor How You Feel**

    What emotions come up as you reflect on this moment? Anger? Disappointment? Hurt? Resentment? Fear? Every feeling is valid. Pay attention to not only your emotions, but also what's happening in your body. Your body isn't just reacting—it's trying to guide you toward what needs your attention.

- **Choose Your Next Move**

    What's one small action you can take to reclaim your power? Maybe it's:
    - Setting a boundary with someone who has overstepped.

- Writing out your thoughts to process your emotions.
- Having a conversation to express how you feel.
- Letting go of something that no longer serves you.

Courage isn't about doing everything at once—it's about taking one step in the direction of self-trust.

- **Take the Step**

    Do the damn thing. Yes, it's going to feel uncomfortable, courage always does. But remind yourself: This isn't about how the other person responds. This is about showing up for you. Courage is the act of honoring yourself, even when it feels unfamiliar. Even when it's scary. Even when it's messy.

Pause and Reflect

Once you've taken that first step, check in with yourself:

- How did it feel to stand up for yourself?
- What did you learn about yourself in the process?
- What would it look like to practice courage again tomorrow?

Even if it wasn't perfect, you proved to yourself that you can do hard things.

Courage is a Daily Decision

Courage isn't about fixing everything in one move. It's about deciding, moment by moment, to honor yourself.

So, take a step. Start small. But keep going.

You've got this.

***

Courage isn't about being fearless—it's about choosing to stand in your truth, even when fear and discomfort are breathing down your neck. It's about showing up for yourself because you're done waiting for someone else to do it for you.

You've spent enough time prioritizing other people's needs, comfort, and opinions over your own. You've swallowed your truth to keep the peace, softened your voice to avoid conflict, and let your boundaries bend to keep others comfortable.

But now? **It's your turn.**

Courage isn't found in grand, dramatic gestures. It lives in the small, everyday choices—the moments when you decide to speak up, hold your ground, finally say, "This is what I need." These decisions might not seem monumental in the moment, but they are. They're the ones that change your life.

It's not going to be easy. You're going to feel scared. You'll second-guess yourself, question whether you're doing the right thing, and wonder if it's even worth it. But here's the truth: Courage doesn't care about perfect timing or perfect words. It doesn't wait for certainty. It just asks you to take one step—messy, uncomfortable, and real.

And when you do? You remind yourself that you're worth it. That your voice matters. That your needs deserve space.

Every small act of courage is a vote for the life you actually want to live. The life that reflects your truth, your values, and your power.

So, keep going. Even when it feels hard. Especially when it feels hard.

Courage is about choosing to show up for yourself when it matters most, even when it's uncomfortable. Even when you're unsure. Even when it feels messy and imperfect.

In this chapter, you've taken a hard look at the moments you stayed quiet, let things slide, or put everyone else's needs ahead of your own. But those moments weren't failures—they were lessons. They revealed where you've been holding back and exposed patterns that no longer serve you.

This isn't about blame—not toward yourself or anyone else. <u>This is about ownership.</u> About recognizing where you've played small, where you've silenced yourself, and choosing to do something different. Because courage isn't just a concept—it's an *action*. It's a daily decision to honor your voice, your values, and your worth.

Courage doesn't always roar—sometimes, it's the quiet decision to do one small thing differently.

1. **Start Small**

    Think of one situation where you've been biting your tongue or ignoring what you need. Take one intentional step to address it—whether that's setting a boundary, saying "no," or simply acknowledging your feelings without dismissing them.

2. **Trust Your Gut**

    Your body always speaks to you. Pay attention to how it reacts to fear or discomfort—that tightness in your chest, that uneasy feeling in your stomach. That's your inner compass trying to guide you. Don't ignore it.

3. **Have the Hard Conversation**

    Pick one person or situation where things feel out of alignment. Revisit the reflection prompts and examples from earlier in this chapter to ground yourself, then speak your truth—even if it's just a simple, honest statement of how you feel.

4. **Acknowledge Your Growth**

    Every single time you choose courage over comfort, you're building a stronger, more aligned version of yourself. Celebrate that—it matters. Your courage matters. You matter.

Courage is essential, but courage without compassion can feel harsh. And compassion without courage? It can keep you stuck.

As we move forward, you'll learn how these two forces work together. Compassion softens courage, and courage strengthens compassion. When combined, they create a life where you show up fully, honestly, and unapologetically.

You're already stepping into that version of yourself.

Keep going.

Notes

These pages are for you—your reflections, breakthroughs, questions, and reminders.
Write what you need to say. Cross it out. Rewrite it.
This is your space to be messy, honest, and free.

_____

_____

_____

_____

_____

_____

_____

_____

_____

_____

_____

_____

_____

_____

_____

Chapter Five

Compassion: Beyond Judgment: Choosing Compassion Over Criticism

Compassion is more than kindness—it's the radical act of not only seeing but honoring the humanity in ourselves and others. It's easy to extend understanding when we see someone else struggling. We instinctively offer a reassuring word, a gentle touch, or even a knowing look that says, *I see you. I understand.* But when the struggle is our own, why do we often respond with criticism instead of care?

For those of us who have spent years prioritizing others, self-compassion can feel foreign—like an indulgence we haven't yet earned. We hold ourselves to impossible standards, believing that worth is something to be proven, not something inherent. We extend grace to everyone except the one person who needs it the most: ourselves.

Time to get honest—being hard on yourself has never made you better, only more exhausted. Compassion is not weakness; it's an act of courage. It's the ability to acknowledge mistakes without turning them into weapons against ourselves. It's the willingness to set boundaries, to rest, to forgive, to recognize that struggle does not make us unworthy—it makes us human.

The world teaches you that being tough on yourself is the path to success. But what if we have it backward? What if true growth comes not from self-punishment, but from self- acceptance? What if the most transformative thing you can do is offer yourself the same compassion you so easily give to others?

In this chapter, we'll explore what it means to embrace compassion as a strength, instead of a weakness. We'll unpack the cost of self-criticism, the freedom of self-kindness, and how choosing compassion—especially for yourself—is a big key to breaking free from cycles of doubt and shame. Because saving yourself starts with giving yourself grace.

***

You know that moment when you see someone struggling, and instead of judgment, your first instinct is to reach out with kindness? Maybe it's a friend going through a tough time, a stranger who looks like they need a little grace, or even a previous version of yourself—the one who didn't know what you know now. That instinct. That's compassion in action. It's the bridge that connects understanding to action, turning empathy into something tangible.

Compassion isn't just about how we treat others. It's about how we treat ourselves. And for those of us who've spent years being everything for everyone else, self-compassion can feel like an afterthought—something we extend to others but never claim for ourselves.

But be real—offering yourself compassion isn't easy. You've been conditioned to believe that worth is earned, that mistakes define you, and that being hard on yourself is the only way to grow. And for those of us used to overdelivering or avoiding disappointment, compassion can feel almost selfish. Because what happens when you finally show yourself kindness? What if it means setting boundaries? What if it means saying no? What if it means forgiving yourself for all the times you didn't know better?

That's the fear that keeps us stuck.

But compassion isn't weakness—it's what allows us to face our pain without letting it define us.

It's the courage to acknowledge our struggles without letting them define us.

It's the grace to embrace our humanity instead of punishing ourselves for it.

It's the radical decision to be on your own side.

The Day I Chose to Show Myself Grace

For a large part of my adult life, I carried an unbearable weight—a quiet, constant shame tied to not being present in my oldest daughter's life. It shaped how I saw myself, how I allowed others to treat me, and how I treated myself. Guilt was my baseline. I believed that because I had failed her, I didn't get to move forward. That I had to keep punishing myself to prove I was sorry. That any joy, rest, or healing I allowed in was somehow a betrayal of the pain I caused.

So I built a life around penance. I overperformed. I gave relentlessly. I made myself small. And I told myself it was noble.

But one day, in what seemed like an ordinary conversation with my daughter, something shifted. We were talking—not about the past, but about the now—and I realized I didn't recognize the version of myself I was still punishing. She didn't exist anymore.

That was the moment I felt something I hadn't in a long time: power.

Not the kind of power that dominates a room, but the kind that roots you to the truth. I had already done the inner work. I had faced my past. I had apologized. I had rebuilt. And in that moment, I finally saw that I was no longer the woman who abandoned her. I was the woman who came back for herself.

I still have deep empathy for my daughter's pain. I always will. But I also realized that holding on to guilt wasn't making me a better mother—it was making me a prisoner to who I used to be.

That day, I chose something different.

I chose grace.

Grace to acknowledge that I can't change the past.

Grace to stop performing worthiness.

Grace to love myself, even when the shame whispers I don't deserve it.

It wasn't a finish line—it was a beginning. A reclamation. A reminder that even after the deepest rupture, healing is still mine to claim.

The Cost of Self-Criticism

Think about all the times you've spoken to yourself in ways you'd never speak to someone else. The internal monologue that tells you you're not enough. The shame that creeps in when you fall short of impossible standards. The weight of carrying past mistakes as if they define your future. That harsh inner voice. That's the cost of not having compassion for yourself. It erodes your confidence, drains your energy, and keeps you in cycles of self-doubt and guilt.

When you don't practice self-compassion, you rely on external validation to determine your worth. You push yourself past exhaustion. You hold onto guilt long after the lesson has been learned. You demand perfection instead of progress. But compassion allows you to extend yourself the same grace you so freely give others. It lets you rest. It lets you breathe. It lets you be.

Figuring out how to treat yourself can be difficult. But you can begin by shifting the way you speak to yourself:

- Instead of "I should have known better," try "I did the best I could with what I knew."
- Instead of "I always mess things up," try "I am learning and growing, just like everyone else."
- Instead of "I don't deserve rest," try "I am worthy of care, just as I am."
- Instead of "I have to prove my worth," try "I am already enough."

Compassion isn't about making excuses—it's about making room. Room to grow, to heal, to be imperfect, and still be worthy. It's about recognizing that struggle is part of the human experience, and that grace is something we all deserve—including you.

The Power of Compassion

Once you begin to extend yourself compassion, everything changes. You stop defining yourself by past mistakes. You stop internalizing every criticism. You stop measuring your worth by how much you can endure.

And at first, this shift might feel foreign—maybe even uncomfortable. But then? It will liberate you. Because when you truly embrace compassion, you give yourself permission to be human.

You start honoring your needs instead of dismissing them. You stop holding yourself to impossible standards. You begin to trust that you are enough—not because of what you do, but simply because you are.

And that. That is the radical act of saving your damn self.

One of the most powerful ways to shift your perspective and cultivate self-compassion is to ask the right questions—ones that align with **The C6 Blueprint™: Curiosity, Clarity, Courage, Compassion, Care, and Consistency**. These questions invite you to explore yourself with honesty and grace, help you break free from self-judgment and move toward self-acceptance. The kind of thought process that challenges your self-criticism, opens you up to grace, and reminds you of your inherent worth.

Here are a few questions, rooted in **The C6 Blueprint™**, that can transform your self-perception and led you toward healing:

- If I spoke to a loved one the way I speak to myself, how would they feel?
- Who taught me that I had to be perfect to be worthy of kindness?
- What would I say to a friend who was struggling the way I am right now?
- Am I holding onto shame that no longer serves me?
- What if I allowed myself to be enough, right now, as I am?

When I started answering these questions honestly, I realized just how much weight I was been carrying. It was time to confront the harmful narratives that were accepted as truth and gave me permission to rewrite them. When you apply **The C6 Blueprint™** to your self-reflection, you create a powerful framework for growth. Curiosity allows you to question your inner critic without fear. Clarity helps you see what narratives are holding you back. Courage challenges you to rewrite them. Compassion gives you permission to embrace yourself fully. Care ensures that you honor your needs. And <u>Consistency</u> turns self-compassion into a life-long practice—ones that guide you toward healing, self-acceptance, and true compassion.

Compassion isn't just an idea—it's a practice, a choice we make daily in how we treat ourselves and others. It's one thing to understand the concept of self-compassion, but another to actively embody it. What does compassion in action look like? How do we move from intention to practice?

Compassion in Your Daily Life

Practicing compassion starts with small, intentional choices. It's in the moments you:

- Offer yourself grace after making a mistake instead of replaying it over and over.
- Pause before reacting to someone else's frustration and consider what they might be carrying.
- Set a boundary to protect your energy, even when it's uncomfortable.
- Forgive yourself for not knowing what you know now.

It's also about recognizing the ways you show up for others. Compassion is listening without judgment, validating emotions without rushing to fix, and showing kindness even when it's not convenient. It's the commitment to meeting yourself and others where you are, without conditions.

Using The C6 Blueprint™ with Compassion

You've already seen how *The C6 Blueprint*™ invites you back to yourself—principle by principle. When compassion leads the way, those values shift from concepts into lived experience.

It shows up in the way you interrupt harsh self-talk, allow space for rest, and give yourself grace instead of guilt. It's how you soften without collapsing, stay honest without harshness, and hold your humanity without apology.

And the more you embody it, the more your relationships begin to change. You stop shrinking for others' comfort. You stop performing kindness while silencing your truth. You become a living example that compassion and boundaries aren't opposites—they're partners.

This is what it means to live what you believe. And when compassion becomes part of your rhythm, healing stops being a destination—and becomes a way of being

When you begin to practice self-compassion, everything around you shifts—including your relationships. You become more patient, more present, and less reactive. You stop taking everything personally because you've stopped punishing yourself internally. Little by little, you start modeling a different way of being—one where kindness and boundaries don't compete, they *coexist*.

Over time, compassion becomes less of a tool and more of a rhythm. Not just something you do—but who you are.

This is compassion in action: living what you believe, even when it's hard.

It's showing up for yourself with the same care you'd offer someone you love.

And in doing so, you create space—real space—for healing, growth, and connection to thrive.

Take A First Step

Understanding compassion is one thing—but putting it into practice is another. It's easy to say, *I'll be kinder to myself*, but when life gets messy, old habits of self-criticism and doubt creep in. Taking a step toward self-compassion isn't about perfection. It's about choosing, in each moment, to offer yourself grace instead of judgment.

Like any muscle, self-compassion gets stronger the more you use it. It won't happen overnight—but with small, intentional actions, it becomes part of how you move through the world.

- **Notice your inner dialogue.** When you catch yourself in self-criticism, pause and reframe it with kindness.

- **Give yourself permission to be human.** You will make mistakes, have bad days, and feel stuck sometimes. That doesn't make you unworthy—it makes you real.

- **Replace self-punishment with self-care.** Instead of pushing through exhaustion or ignoring your needs, ask: *What would someone who truly cared about me encourage me to do?*

- **Celebrate small wins.** Compassion grows when you acknowledge progress, not just big achievements.

A Commitment to Yourself

Moving toward self-compassion is a commitment—one that no one else can make for you. It's deciding, today, that you will treat yourself with the same care and patience that you offer others. It's understanding that showing up for yourself isn't selfish; it's necessary.

Take a deep breath.

Choose one act of self-compassion today, no matter how small. And then another tomorrow. This is how change begins.

You've come this far, which means something inside you is ready for change. Ready to release the weight of perfectionism, the exhaustion of self-judgment, and the habit of being your own harshest critic. The journey to self-compassion doesn't require a grand gesture or a radical transformation overnight. It begins with one small, courageous choice: Be kind to yourself, even when it feels unnatural.

Every moment is an opportunity to extend compassion, especially to yourself. When you start treating yourself with the same grace you so freely offer the people you love, you open the door to a life of deeper connection, inner peace, and true freedom. You begin to see that self-compassion is not a luxury; it's a necessity. It is the foundation for growth, resilience, and an unshakable sense of self-worth.

This is your invitation to show up for yourself in a way you never have before. To rewrite the inner dialogue that has kept you stuck. To trust that you are enough, exactly as you are. And to walk forward, not in pursuit of perfection, but in pursuit of a life where you are no longer at war with yourself.

Start today. Start now. You are worthy of your own kindness.

Once you begin to extend yourself compassion, everything changes. You stop defining yourself by past mistakes. You stop internalizing every criticism. You stop measuring your worth by how much you can endure.

And at first, that shift might feel foreign—maybe even uncomfortable. But it will liberate you. Because when you truly embrace compassion, you give yourself permission to be human.

You start honoring your needs instead of dismissing them. You stop holding yourself to impossible standards. You begin to trust that you are enough—not because of what you do, but simply because of who you are.

And that? That is the radical act of saving your damn self.

***

Compassion is more than a concept—it transforms how you see yourself and the world around you. When you start offering yourself the grace you extend to others, everything shifts. The weight of self-judgment begins to lift, and in its place, you discover a new kind of strength. The strength to embrace your imperfections, set boundaries, and show up for yourself with kindness.

The journey to self-compassion isn't about being perfect—it's about making small, intentional choices that align with your values. It's about replacing self-criticism with curiosity, harshness with care, and doubt with courage. Through **The C6 Blueprint™** you can create a foundation for lasting change.

But this is just the beginning. Soon, we'll explore how to take the self-compassion you've cultivated and channel it into deeper self-care, intentional boundaries, and create a life that truly reflects your values. Compassion is the doorway to deeper transformation, a key step in breaking free from old narratives and stepping into the life you truly deserve. As you move forward, remember that every moment is an opportunity to choose grace over judgment, healing over shame, and authenticity over perfection.

Notes

These pages are for you—your reflections, breakthroughs, questions, and reminders.

Write what you need to say. Cross it out. Rewrite it.

This is your space to be messy, honest, and free.

_____

_____

_____

_____

_____

_____

_____

_____

_____

_____

_____

_____

_____

_____

Chapter Six

Care: Treating Yourself Like the Treasure You Are

Care is often misunderstood. We often associate it with obligation—caring for others, fulfilling responsibilities, meeting expectations. But at its core, care is a radical act of self-preservation, a statement that says, *I matter too.* In The C6 Blueprint™, care is not just about extending kindness outward; it's about recognizing that true well-being starts from within.

Because you have spent years prioritizing everyone else's needs over your own, self-care can feel like a foreign concept. Many of us have been conditioned to believe that self-care is indulgent or that putting ourselves first is selfish. But real care—the kind that nurtures, restores, and strengthens—allows us to show up in our lives as whole, healthy, and fully present beings.

Care is not just about what you do; it's about how you do it. It's in the way you set boundaries to protect your energy. It's in the way you speak to yourself, the decisions you make, and the environments you create.

When you practice care intentionally, you shift from surviving to thriving.

Through the lens of The C6 Blueprint™:

- **Curiosity** helps you explore what care actually looks like for you, rather than what society dictates.
- **Clarity** allows you to see where you've neglected your own needs.
- **Courage** pushes you to prioritize yourself, even when it feels uncomfortable.
- **Compassion** reminds you that you are deserving of the same kindness you offer others.
- **Care** becomes a conscious, daily practice instead of an afterthought.
- **Consistency** ensures that care is not just a one-time act, but a lifelong commitment.

It's time to redefine care on your own terms. It's time to dismantle the belief that prioritizing yourself is selfish and embrace the truth: When you care for yourself, you expand your capacity to care for everything else in your life.

Let's step into this journey together.

Choosing Myself

People like you and I barely have time to think of ourselves. There are so many competing obligations and demands on our time that sometimes, just being able to sleep soundly feels like enough. We often disregard that uncomfortableness in our gut telling us it's time to do something different.

For me, that discomfort turned into a quiet desire to disappear. I didn't know what I needed to feel whole, and that confusion created even more chaos inside me. Instead of releasing the weight, I absorbed it. My mind became a battlefield—I was constantly fighting myself, and it was exhausting. Over time, I lost track of the exact moments things unraveled. But the pattern was always the same: pushing through the exhaustion until I collapsed into isolation, retreating into what I now call social-scaping—disconnecting from everything in a desperate attempt to find relief.

I finally started paying attention when I realized none of my so-called self-care tools were working. I was following what I had seen others do—buying journals, reading self-help books, meditating—but none of it stuck. Because I was trying to copy someone else's version of self-care instead of discovering what actually worked for me.

Then, one day at work, a co-worker asked me a simple question: *How do you take care of yourself?*

I nearly burst into tears. Because I didn't know the answer.

Outside of consuming self-help content, I had no idea what real self-care looked like for me. I sat with that question, letting it challenge me instead of running from it. And then I remembered something: I loved to color. As a kid, coloring was my escape, my joy, my way of grounding myself. When had I stopped?

That realization cracked something open. I farmed out my self-care by pouring into everyone else, hoping that care would return to me. No wonder I was always tired, in pain, and filled with resentment—I had abandoned myself. I was doing all the things—showing up for work, supporting friends and family, saying yes to every request, and keeping everything moving. From the outside, it looked like I had it all together. But inside? I was running on fumes.

After weeks of pushing through exhaustion, I found myself sitting in my car outside the grocery store, unable to move. I wasn't crying. I wasn't panicked. I was just… empty. My body had reached its limit, and my mind was following.

That moment scared me. Because if I didn't even have the energy to walk into a store and pick up groceries, what else was I losing? My patience had been wearing thin with the people I loved. My creativity had vanished. I was resenting the very things I once enjoyed.

The Moment Everything Changed

I did something I had never done before—I left.

I sent a message to the people in my household, letting them know I needed something different. I needed space. I needed safety. I needed joy. And I was done waiting for things to shift on their own. I didn't explain where I was going. I just said, *"I'll be back when I get back."*

I booked an Airbnb by the beach, packed a bag, and left. I had every intention of doing something structured—journaling, coloring, sitting in stillness by the water. But once I arrived, none of that happened. I didn't walk the shoreline or unpack the plans. Instead, I slept. I logged off social media. I curled up in pajamas and watched cartoons. And for the first time in what felt like forever, I felt peace.

In those two days, I learned something life-changing: *rest is revolutionary.* Self-care isn't selfish—it's self-full. I still had to fight the belief that slowing down meant I was failing. But the truth was undeniable—if I kept running myself into the ground, I wouldn't have anything left to give. Not to others. And not to myself.

That's why I had to start asking myself different questions—ones that challenged the patterns I had accepted as normal:

- Why are you treating your own needs as an afterthought?

- Who taught you that being exhausted was a sign of success?

- What would it look like to give yourself the same care you give everyone else?

Through curiosity, you start to understand that self-care isn't about indulgence—it is about survival. Through clarity, you can see how deeply you have neglected your own well-being. Through courage, you can make changes that feel uncomfortable at first—saying no, setting boundaries, resting without guilt.

Self-Care on Your Terms

I spent so much time trying to do self-care the right way that I missed the point entirely. Care isn't about checking off a list of trendy activities—it's about doing what replenishes you. For me, it was rest, solitude, and coloring. For you, it might be movement, community, or creativity.

The C6 Blueprint™ helped me see that care isn't passive; it's an active commitment to myself. Curiosity helped me explore what I truly needed. Clarity allowed me to recognize my patterns of neglect. Courage helped me step away from the pressure to perform self-care for others and do what actually worked for me. Compassion reminded me that I deserved the same grace I offered to others. Care became a conscious, daily practice instead of an afterthought. Consistency ensured that self-care wasn't just an emergency response, but a foundation for how I lived my life.

That trip was a turning point. Not because it fixed everything, but because it showed me what was possible when I put myself first. It's the hard decisions, the daily choices that protect your energy and well-being. It's recognizing when you're depleted and doing something about it before you hit the point of collapse. It's:

- Setting boundaries that protect your peace.
- Speaking to yourself with kindness instead of criticism.
- Nourishing your body with rest, food, and movement that fuels you.
- Creating spaces—physically and emotionally—that support your well-being.
- Allowing yourself joy without feeling like you have to earn it.

The C6 Blueprint™ will show you that care isn't passive; it's an active commitment to yourself. Compassion reminds you that you deserve grace, just like anyone else. And consistency turns self-care from an emergency response into a daily practice.

You are Worth the Care You Give Others

Self-care is still a work in progress. Some days, I fall back into old habits, thinking I need to earn rest or that taking time for myself is selfish. But then I remember that breaking patterns takes time.

I think back to that moment when my co-worker asked me how I took care of myself, and I had no answer. Now, I do. I listen to my body. I protect my peace. I create space for joy without guilt. And when life gets overwhelming, I no longer wait until I'm on the verge of breaking before I give myself what I need.

So, I ask you: *How do you take care of yourself?*

If you don't know the answer yet, that's okay. But let this be your moment—the one where you stop putting yourself last and start treating yourself like someone worth caring for. Because the truth is, you always have been. Remind yourself that when you take care of yourself, you show up better for the people and things you care about.

This chapter isn't just about understanding care—it's about reclaiming it. It's about rewriting the belief that your worth is tied to how much you do for others and instead recognizing that you are just as deserving of care as anyone else.

So, ask yourself: *How can you start showing yourself the care you so freely give to others?* Because the most radical thing you can do is believe that *you matter too.*

Self-care isn't a checklist, a trend, or something you "earn" only after exhaustion sets in. It's a deeply personal, ongoing practice of choosing yourself—over and over again. True self-care isn't about what looks good on the outside; it's about what nourishes you from within.

Take a moment to reflect on your relationship with care using these prompts:

- **Curiosity:** What are the activities, moments, or experiences that genuinely bring me peace and joy? Have I been making time for them, or have they been pushed to the side?
- **Clarity:** Where in my life have I consistently neglected my own needs? What patterns of self-neglect do I recognize?
- **Courage:** What is one uncomfortable but necessary boundary I need to set to protect my well-being? What's stopping me from enforcing it?
- **Compassion:** How do I speak to myself when I'm struggling? Would I say those same words to a friend? If not, how can I shift my self-talk to be more supportive?
- **Care:** What daily or weekly practices can I put in place to nourish my body, mind, and spirit—without waiting until I'm depleted?

- **Consistency:** What small act of self-care can I commit to, starting today, to create a lasting habit of honoring myself?

As you reflect, release judgment. There is no "right" way to care for yourself—only what feels right to you. Let this be your invitation to redefine self-care in a way that truly serves you, not just today, but always.

Making Moves Using Care

Understanding the importance of self-care is one thing—implementing it is another. Care isn't just about recognizing that you deserve rest and nourishment; it's about taking steps to intentional integrate it into your daily life. Here are some ways to put care into action, guided by The C6 Blueprint™:

- **Curiosity: Discover What Truly Replenishes You**
    - Explore different forms of self-care without pressure. Try activities that spark joy, relaxation, or creativity—whether it's reading, cooking, movement, or solitude.
    - Ask yourself: *What activities make me feel alive, at peace, or restored?*

- Release any preconceived notions about what self-care should look like and focus on what feels right.

- **Clarity: Identify What's Draining You**
  - Reflect on where your time and energy are being spent. Are there obligations, relationships, or habits that leave you feeling depleted?
  - Track your emotions throughout the day. When do you feel most energized? When do you feel the most exhausted?
  - Ask yourself: *What would change if I prioritized my well-being as much as I do my responsibilities?*

- **Courage: Set Boundaries Without Guilt**
  - Boundaries are essential acts of care. Whether it's limiting your availability, saying no to unnecessary obligations, or creating personal space, protecting your energy is a necessity, not a luxury.
  - Practice saying no with confidence. A simple, *"I can't commit to that right now"* is enough.
  - Remember: Setting boundaries doesn't make you selfish—it makes you sustainable.

- **Compassion: Speak to Yourself with Kindness**
    - Pay attention to your inner dialogue. When you catch self-criticism, pause and reframe it as you would for a friend.
    - Instead of *"I should be doing more,"* try *"I am doing enough."*
    - Allow yourself grace in the moments when you fall back into old habits. Self-care is not about perfection—it's about consistency.

- **Care: Create Nonnegotiable Rituals**
    - Establish a daily or weekly practice that prioritizes your well-being. It can be as simple as a morning stretch, an evening gratitude journal, or scheduling time to rest.
    - Make self-care nonnegotiable. Treat it like you would any other commitment—because your well-being deserves the same level of importance.
    - Ask yourself: *What is one small act of care I can commit to today?*

- **Consistency: Build a Sustainable Practice**
    - The key to lasting self-care is making it a lifestyle. Start small and build from there.
    - Identify one self-care practice you can implement daily and one you can prioritize weekly.
    - Be patient with yourself. Developing a consistent self-care routine takes time, but every step matters.

Making the Shift

Self-care is not about escaping life—it's about creating a life that doesn't require you to constantly need to escape. When you actively practice care, you begin to shift from merely surviving to truly thriving. You no longer wait until burnout forces you to rest; you learn to integrate rest and restoration into your daily existence.

The C6 Blueprint™ isn't just a framework—it's a way to reimagine care as an active, intentional choice. It's recognizing that your well-being is just as important as the roles you fill and the people you support.

So, where do you begin? Choose one area from The C6 Blueprint™ and take one small action today. Because the most radical act of self-care is deciding that you are worth the effort.

Understanding self-care is one thing—committing to it is another. If you've spent years prioritizing everyone and everything else, making yourself a priority may feel uncomfortable at first. But self-care isn't about making a drastic change overnight; it starts with one small, intentional action.

You don't need an elaborate routine or a perfectly curated wellness plan to begin. Pay attention to yourself—your energy levels, emotions, and physical needs. Are you tired? Overwhelmed? Irritable? Your body and mind are always communicating what they need—it's time to listen.

- **Check in with yourself daily.** Ask: *How am I feeling right now? What do I need in this moment?*
- **Commit to one small act of care.** Whether it's drinking more water, stepping outside for fresh air, taking five minutes to breathe, or saying no to something draining—start somewhere.
- **Make self-care nonnegotiable.** Treat it as essential as your job, relationships, and responsibilities—because it is.

Give Yourself Permission

Many of us have internalized the belief that self-care is selfish, indulgent, or unproductive. Challenge that mindset. Taking care of yourself doesn't take away from anyone else—it allows you to show up more fully in all areas of your life.

- **Release the guilt.** You don't need to earn rest. You don't have to justify taking time for yourself.
- **Stop comparing your self-care to others.** What works for someone else may not work for you, and that's okay.
- **Remind yourself that prioritizing your well-being benefits everyone in your life.** You can't pour from an empty cup, and caring for yourself allows you to be more present, engaged, and intentional in everything else you do.

Change doesn't happen overnight, and it doesn't have to. Every small act of self-care builds the foundation for a life where you are cared for—not just by others, but by you.

Start where you are. Commit to one thing today—because you are worth the effort.

Embracing Care and Looking Ahead

Self-care isn't about adding more to your to-do list—it's about restructuring your life in a way that sustains you.

By now, you've seen how The C6 Blueprint™ can help redefine care as an intentional practice rather than an afterthought.

- <u>Curiosity</u> helps you explore what care actually means for you.
- <u>Clarity</u> gives you insight into where you've been neglecting yourself.
- <u>Courage</u> pushes you to set boundaries and prioritize your needs.
- <u>Compassion</u> reminds you that you are deserving of the same kindness you extend to others.
- <u>Care</u> is reframed as a necessity, not a luxury.
- <u>Consistency</u> is the key to making self-care a sustainable practice.

As you move forward, think about how you will continue to integrate care into your daily life. Your journey doesn't end here. It's an ongoing commitment to yourself, one that will evolve with time.

Next, we'll explore the power of consistency—an integral piece of The C6 Blueprint™. Because care is not just about recognizing what you need; it's about showing up for yourself, again and again, with intention and love.

Self-care is deeply personal. It's not a checklist or a one-size-fits-all solution—it's about discovering what truly nourishes and sustains you. Use these prompts to reflect on your relationship with care and what it looks like for you:

- **Curiosity:** What are the things that genuinely bring me peace and joy? Have I been making time for them?
- **Clarity:** Where in my life have I neglected my own needs? What patterns of self- neglect have I noticed?
- **Courage:** What is one uncomfortable but necessary boundary I need to set to protect my well-being?
- **Compassion:** How do I speak to myself when I'm struggling? Would I talk to a friend the same way?
- **Care:** What daily or weekly practices can I put in place to nourish my body, mind, and spirit?
- **Consistency:** What small act of self-care can I commit to, starting today, to create a lasting habit?

Reflect on your answers without judgment. This is your invitation to re-define care in a way that feels right for you.

Notes

These pages are for you—your reflections, breakthroughs, questions, and reminders.

Write what you need to say. Cross it out. Rewrite it.

This is your space to be messy, honest, and free.

_____

_____

_____

_____

_____

_____

_____

_____

_____

_____

_____

_____

_____

_____

_____

_____

Chapter Seven

Consistency: Building the Foundation for Lasting Change

If you're reading this book and feeling "called out," no, friend—this is a gentle *call in*. A reminder that growth isn't about collecting wisdom; it's about consistently applying it.

Let's start with this: Stop buying new journals and planners every time the metaphorical sun in your life shines. This is a sign of inconsistency. Stop seeking answers from spiritual and religious leaders over and over when you already received guidance the first time—trust yourself enough to follow through. Stop picking up a new self-help book (except this one—put it in your purse) every time you feel pulled to grow and instead, commit to consistent action.

Stop escaping into distractions when things get hard or abandoning goals the moment they lose their shine. And, most importantly, stop lecturing others on their journeys while actively taking none of the advice yourself.

Consistency is what separates insight from transformation. It's not about making perfect choices every day; it's about making intentional choices *over time*. Through The C6

Blueprint™, you've learned to cultivate curiosity, clarity, courage, compassion, and care—but without consistency, these lessons don't become habits.

Consistency isn't just about making choices—it's about making a decision. A choice can be temporary, something you pick up and put down. But a decision is a commitment, a line in the sand. One that says, "This is who I am now." If you've been wading in and out of growth, it's time to decide. Decide that you will follow through, even when motivation fades. Decide that you will stop starting over and start following through. Decide that your evolution is worth the effort.

This chapter is an invitation to stop seeking the next best thing and start showing up for the life you've been building.

Let's get to work.

When It's Time to Take Action

I can't wrap this into a neat, tidy story because, honestly, this battle has been real for a long time. Not only did I celebrate being a sponge, a lifelong learner, and a student of growth—I was also more malleable than I wanted to be. I absorbed everything, yet I wasn't doing anything. I wasn't dealing with the "why" behind my inaction. And until you dealt with that, you can't move forward.

I received a divine call in 2017 to complete a workbook. I actually created it—but never showed it to anyone. I convinced myself it wasn't enough. It needed more. So it sat there, unfinished, unseen, collecting digital dust. Or what about the certification I *needed*—until it was time to take the exam? I chickened out, paralyzed by fear. And then there were the expectations and boundaries I set, only to let them slip away when enforcing them got uncomfortable.

If you see yourself in these stories, don't judge yourself. Instead, recognize the *gift* in realizing where you've been inconsistent—and do something about it. Because here's a realization I had to face: Using fear as my guidepost, choosing what was easy or socially acceptable, and staying under the radar kept me small. It kept me boxed into a reality I was quickly outgrowing.

I felt shame every time I said, next time, knowing deep down that there wouldn't be a next time if I didn't make it happen. I made excuses for people violating my boundaries, blaming them instead of holding myself accountable for not enforcing them. I forgot the most critical truth: I am the common denominator in every situation involving me. People will always do what is best for *them*—so why wasn't I doing what was best for me?

Understanding that truth was a wake-up call. It forced me to examine my behaviors, my patterns, and even my anti-gifts—the strengths I overused to the point that they started harming me instead of helping me. My inconsistency wasn't just about not finishing tasks. It was about being unreliable to myself, creating chaos where there didn't need to be any.

Then it hit me—consistency isn't just about discipline or routines. It is about trusting myself. Every time I abandoned a project, failed to follow through, or let my boundaries slide, I was sending a message to myself that I wasn't trustworthy. That my own word didn't mean anything. And that realization was devastating.

It wasn't just about unfinished workbooks or certifications—I had unknowingly built a pattern of abandoning *myself*. And if I couldn't trust myself to follow through, how could I ever expect to build anything meaningful?

That's when I knew I had to change. I had to stop chasing perfection and start prioritizing

progress. I had to stop waiting for motivation and start relying on commitment. I had to recognize that showing up, even when it felt small and insignificant, was the only way I would ever become the person I envisioned.

So I decided. Not just to try, but to commit. To stop starting over and start following through. To stop gathering knowledge and start applying it. To stop waiting for the perfect moment and start making the current one count.

I made small, deliberate changes. I finished a project and shared it, even when it wasn't perfect. I stuck to a boundary, even when it was uncomfortable. I held myself accountable, even when it would have been easier to let it slide. And each time I did, I proved to myself that I could be consistent. That I could be relied upon—not just by others, but by me.

And that's when everything will start shifting. The confidence you thought you lacked. It isn't something you needed to *find*—it is something you need to *build*. And you can only build it by proving to yourself, over and over, that you were someone who follows through.

The harsh reality? Future me wasn't coming to save me. I had to take actions to become her. This chapter is about that decision. The one that changes everything.

Make A Commitment

Consistency is the foundation of self-trust. Without it, even the best intentions fall apart. If you've struggled with follow-through in different areas of your life, you're not alone. But to change, you have to first recognize where and why inconsistency shows up. Take time to reflect on these questions:

- <u>Where in my life have I struggled to stay consistent?</u> Is it in personal habits, work, relationships, or setting boundaries?
- <u>What patterns of inconsistency do I notice?</u> Do I start strong and lose interest? Do I get discouraged when progress feels slow?

- <u>What emotions come up when I think about committing to consistency?</u> Fear of failure? Doubt? Resistance?

- <u>How has inconsistency impacted my self-trust?</u> Have I made promises to myself that I didn't keep? How has that affected my confidence?

- <u>When have I been consistent in the past?</u> What allowed me to stay committed in those moments?

- <u>What excuses do I make for not following through?</u> How do I justify inconsistency to myself?

- <u>What small action can I commit to right now to start building consistency?</u>

Recognizing your patterns is the first step toward breaking them. Sit with these questions, journal your thoughts, and use your answers to create a clear path forward.

Consistency isn't about willpower or waiting for the perfect moment—it's about creating systems and mindsets that make follow-through easier. When you shift from relying on motivation to committing to action, you remove the emotional resistance that often leads to procrastination. Here's how you can make consistency a habit that sticks:

- **Lower the Bar for Success**

  One of the biggest obstacles to consistency is setting goals that are too ambitious too quick. Instead of aiming for massive changes overnight, focus on small, manageable steps. If your goal is to exercise, start with five minutes a day instead of an hour. If you want to read more, commit to a single page before bed. When you make the task easier, you remove the resistance that often leads to inaction. Progress, no matter how small, builds momentum.

- **Track Your Progress**

  What gets measured, gets maintained. Keeping track of your consistency—whether through a habit tracker, journal, or calendar—provides visible proof of your progress. Seeing a streak of completed tasks makes you more likely to continue. If you miss a day, don't abandon the habit—simply start again. The key to long-term success isn't never failing; it's never quitting.

- **Attach New Habits to Existing Routines**

  One of the easiest ways to maintain consistency is to link new habits to something you already do. If you want to journal, do it while drinking your morning coffee. If you want to meditate, make it the first thing you do after brushing your teeth. When new actions have a clear anchor, they become second nature.

- **Shift From Motivation to Commitment**

    Motivation is unreliable—it comes and goes. Commitment, however, is a decision you make every day. The difference between people who succeed and those who struggle isn't that they feel motivated all the time—it's that they act even when they don't feel like it. When you remove the option to quit, consistency becomes a natural part of your life.

- **Build Self-Trust Through Follow-Through**

    Every time you follow through on a commitment to yourself, you reinforce the belief that you can be trusted. If you constantly break promises to yourself, you subconsciously reinforce self-doubt. The solution? Start small. Keep one promise today. Then another tomorrow. Over time, these small wins create a foundation of trust in yourself.

Consistency isn't about perfection—it's about persistence. It's about showing up for yourself, even when no one else is watching. When you make following through a habit, success stops being a matter of luck and starts being the result of who you choose to become.

Choices vs. Decisions

The hardest part of building consistency isn't the work itself—it's the decision to start. Too often, we wait for the perfect conditions, the right mood, or some external push to motivate us into action. But the truth is, motivation is fleeting, and a perfect moment doesn't exist. If you want to change, you must decide and act.

Making a choice is easy, but a decision is a commitment. A choice leaves room for doubt, but a decision says: *This is who I am now.* That's the level of clarity and commitment required for real transformation. You are no longer trying—you are doing.

So, if you're ready to stop circling the same patterns, here's what choosing real change might look like in practice:

- **Identify Where You Need Consistency**

    Instead of overwhelming yourself with multiple changes, focus on one area in your life where inconsistency has held you back. Have you been starting projects but never finishing them? Do you struggle to maintain boundaries, prioritize self-care, or follow through on commitments? Pick one thing to improve first.

If you try to overhaul everything at once, you'll likely get overwhelmed and revert to old patterns. Start with something that will make a meaningful impact. It could be waking up at the same time each morning, committing to a small creative project, or enforcing a personal boundary.

- **Lower the Barrier to Action**

    Perfectionism often leads to procrastination. If the goal feels too big, your mind will resist it. The solution? Make your first step so small it feels impossible to fail.

    - o If you want to read more, commit to reading one page a day.
    - o If you want to be more active, start with five minutes of stretching.
    - o If you want to journal, start by writing a single sentence each night.

    Consistency isn't built by grand gestures but by small, repeated actions. The goal is to prove to yourself that you can follow through. Once you see small wins, you'll be more likely to keep going.

- **Create a Seven-Day Challenge**

    Long-term commitments can feel overwhelming, but a seven-day challenge creates immediate momentum. Tell yourself: *"For the next seven days, I will follow through on my commitment every day. No excuses, no negotiations."*

This short timeframe removes the pressure of a life-long habit but is long enough to build traction. After seven days, you'll have proof that you can be consistent. Then, extend it to two weeks, a month, and beyond.

- **Build Accountability Into Your Plan**

    When no one knows about your commitment, it's easy to let yourself off the hook. That's why accountability is key.

    - Write your goal down and put it somewhere visible.
    - Track your progress in a habit tracker or journal.
    - Tell a friend or mentor about your commitment.

    When you hold yourself accountable, you remove the option to quit quietly. You're more likely to show up when you know you'll have to check in with someone—or even if it's just yourself.

- **Evaluate and Adjust**

    At the end of your seven-day challenge, take time to reflect:

    - What worked well?
    - What challenges did you face?
    - Were there moments you wanted to quit? What triggered that feeling?

    Adjust as needed, but don't stop. The goal isn't perfection—it's progress. If something didn't work, tweak it rather than abandon it.

Consistency is Who You Become

Your future self isn't waiting for the right conditions—she's waiting for you to take the first step.

Once you decide and act, you'll realize that showing up consistently is the key to unlocking everything you've ever wanted. The transformation you desire isn't in the next book, the next class, or the next *opportunity*—it's in your daily actions, repeated over time.

So, what's the small step you're committing to today? Decide. Then act.

Consistency is not about grinding yourself into exhaustion—it's about honoring your commitments to yourself. It's about deciding, once and for all, that you are worth the effort.

Every time you show up, even in the smallest of ways, you reinforce a powerful truth: You can be trusted. You are no longer waiting for motivation to strike. You are no longer waiting for the perfect conditions to align. You are no longer hoping that a future version of yourself will magically appear and fix things for you.

Instead, you are becoming that person now—through action.

Consistency is the bridge between who you are today and who you *want* to be. And every single step you take across that bridge strengthens your self-trust, resilience, and ability to create the life you actually *deserve*.

This isn't about adding more to your plate. It's not about doing *everything*—it's about doing what matters. It's about following through on the promises you make to yourself, no matter how small.

So start today. Show up in one way, no matter how insignificant it may seem. Then do it again tomorrow. And the next day.

One decision at a time. One action at a time. One version of you stepping forward at a time.

The person you're striving to become? She's already within you—waiting on the other side of consistency. It's time to go get her.

Consistency is the key that turns knowledge into transformation. Without it, everything you've learned— about curiosity, clarity, courage, compassion, and care—

remains just a theory. But with consistency, these principles become a part of your identity, not just things you practice when it's convenient or when motivation is high. They become the foundation of how you move through life.

You've now taken a deep dive into the power of deciding, committing, and following through. You've learned that consistency isn't about perfection—it's about showing up, even in small ways, over and over again.

So, the question now is: *What happens next?*

The answer? **You keep going.**

It's easy to start strong, to feel energized by the promise of a fresh beginning. But real transformation happens in the middle—when the excitement fades, when obstacles arise, when old patterns try to pull you back. That's where true growth is tested. And in the next chapter, we're going to explore exactly that.

Because consistency isn't just about starting—it's about staying. It's about trusting yourself enough to follow through, even when the process feels slow.

You've already proven you can do hard things. Now it's time to make them a part of who you are.

Let's move forward.

Notes

These pages are for you—your reflections, breakthroughs, questions, and reminders.
Write what you need to say. Cross it out. Rewrite it.
This is your space to be messy, honest, and free.

_____

_____

_____

_____

_____

_____

_____

_____

_____

_____

_____

_____

_____

_____

_____

_____

_____

Chapter Eight

Your INNEREVOLUTION in Real Life: Stories, Shifts, and the Space to Begin Again

Story: Unwritten by Design

Nia was told who she was before she ever had the chance to find out for herself.

The world had already written her story in ink—poverty, teen pregnancy, failure. Another girl destined to "end up just like her mama."

They said she'd get hooked on drugs. Drop out. Live with regret.

They weren't all strangers either. Some of the same people who were "supposed to help" spoke about her mother with disgust behind closed doors. And Nia heard every word.

So she learned shame early. Wore it like skin. Got used to being last picked, called ugly, bullied, and alone—even in a room full of people.

And still… Nia listened.

Not to herself, but to others. Obsessed with their stories. Their needs. Their expectations.

She became a master of escaping her own life by disappearing into theirs. Withdrawn. Depressed. But driven.

Nia made it her mission to prove them wrong. And she did.

She climbed, achieved, and became the very definition of success—on paper.

But no matter how high she rose, she couldn't outrun the echo of those first words: *"This is who you are."*

They haunted her.

Until one day, instead of running from that voice, she got curious about it.

Whose voice is that?

What if it's not mine?

What if I never needed to prove them wrong, I just needed to get to know myself?

That's when everything shifted.

That's when Nia began.

Blueprint Breakdown: Curiosity in Action

Curiosity isn't always loud. Sometimes it whispers—just loud enough to interrupt the noise.

For years, **Layah** had been living in reaction to other people's perceptions—fueled by shame, driven by doubt, and measuring her worth by how far she could distance herself from the story they gave her.

But curiosity changed the question from *"How do I prove them wrong?"* to *"Who do I want to be if no one else is watching?"*

Curiosity doesn't ask for the right answer. It creates space for the real one.

It's not about fixing or performing. It's about seeing. And what **Layah** finally saw was herself.

Help See Yourself Clearly

- When did you first learn to question who you were?
- Whose voice is loudest in your head—and does it belong to you?
- Have you been living to prove someone wrong… or trying to prove that you're enough?
- What would it feel like to get curious about your truth instead of running from your past?

Try This: INNEREVOLUTION in Action

For the next 24 hours, practice this radical shift:

Any time you hear an old story in your head— *"You'll never be good enough," "This is just who I am," "No one cares anyway"*— pause and ask: *"What else might be true?"*

You don't need an answer. Just the willingness to ask.

Anchor It: A Truth to Carry

"I don't need to fight to become who I am. I just need the courage to ask who I've always been beneath the noise."

Story: The Mirror Was Never Broken

Maya didn't think of herself as lost—she thought of herself as exhausted.

She was doing *all the things*. Showing up. Smiling. Getting shit done.

Her calendar stayed full, her inbox was a battlefield, and her weekends were booked with back-to-back obligations she never actually agreed to—she just didn't say no fast enough.

But something started to feel...off.

She couldn't name it, but it was like her own life was happening in a language she no longer understood.

One day, she sat in her car, engine off, 30 minutes late to a meeting that wasn't even hers to lead. And instead of rushing in, she just sat.

No music. No fake pep talk. Just stillness. And in that stillness, a question came: *"What am I pretending not to know?"*

The answer hit hard: **Everything.**

She'd been pretending not to know that she didn't want to be in that relationship. Pretending not to know she was working a job that looked good but felt like a slow death. Pretending not to know that every "yes" was costing her something she could no longer afford— herself.

Maya didn't need more advice. She needed clarity.

So she made space for it. And when she finally looked in the mirror, it was never broken— it was just covered in other people's fingerprints.

Blueprint Breakdown: Clarity in Action

Clarity doesn't come in chaos—it requires room.

And the truth is, many of us keep our lives loud because we're scared of what we'll hear in the quiet. But clarity isn't just about knowing what you want. It's about owning what you don't. It's about realizing that your values, beliefs, vision—don't need a committee to make sense.

For Maya, clarity was the moment she decided to stop outsourcing her knowledge. And for you, it might be the moment you decide to trust the voice that's been whispering all along.

Help See Yourself Clearly

- What are you pretending not to know about your life right now?
- Whose approval are you quietly chasing?
- What decisions would you make if you believed your clarity didn't need validation?
- Are you aligned with what matters—or just busy?

Try This: INNEREVOLUTION in Action

This week, carve out 10 minutes a day for intentional stillness—no music, no scrolling, no distractions.

Ask yourself: *"What truth is waiting for me beneath the noise?"*

Write it down without editing. Let the realness rise.

Anchor It: A Truth to Carry

"My clarity is not up for debate. I don't need permission to know myself."

Story: A Silence That Speaks

There was a time **Imani** thought the worst was behind them.

She had changed—done the work, unlearned the patterns, softened where she used to harden. She was learning to mother differently. With tenderness. With truth.

So when the relationship with her daughter started to feel steady again, she breathed easier. She thought the door to healing was wide open. That they were finally walking through it together.

But healing is never a straight line.

One day, **Imani** was asked a question that, in her gut, she knew wasn't meant to be answered—not because she didn't want to be honest, but because the answer would do more harm than good.

So she paused. She chose silence.

And her daughter chose space.

No contact. No closure. Just... silence.

It gutted her.

But in that stillness, **Imani** faced something even harder than her daughter's absence: the truth. Sometimes people need space to grieve the version of you that hurt them—even if that version no longer exists.

She cried. Raged. Begged God for understanding.

And eventually, she stopped trying to be understood and started understanding.

Understanding her daughter's truth. Her pain. Her boundaries. And understanding her own. The courage it took to change.

The courage it took to not defend herself. The courage to love from a distance and still be accountable for wounds she never meant to cause.

This wasn't about being right. It was about being real.

This is what courage can look like—not fighting back but standing still and staying open.

Even when no one's clapping.

Even when no one's coming back.

Blueprint Breakdown: Courage in Action

Courage doesn't always come with volume.

Sometimes it's quiet, steady, and sounds like:

"I understand."

"I'll be here if and when you're ready."

"I'm still healing, too."

True courage isn't about saving face. It's about facing the parts of yourself that once caused harm—without collapsing into shame or hiding behind pride. It's learning to hold both your growth and your grief in the same hand.

It's realizing that some doors don't close because you're unworthy—they close because healing takes time. And you can still honor yourself while honoring someone else's process That's brave.

Help See Yourself Clearly

- Have you confused being courageous with being in control?

- What would it look like to stay accountable without needing to be forgiven right away?

- Who have you become that deserves acknowledgment—even if no one else sees it yet?

- Are you willing to be misunderstood as you become more whole?

Try This: INNEREVOLUTION in Action

Write a letter to the version of yourself who didn't know better. The one who tried, failed, and is still learning.

Let her know you see her now. That she's forgiven. That her courage didn't go unnoticed.

You don't have to send it. But she needs to hear from you.

Anchor It: A Truth to Carry

"My courage doesn't erase the past—it gives me the strength to live differently now."

Story: The Girl She Buried

Amara thought she was doing better.

After all, she was showing up. Trying harder. Smiling more. Isn't that what growth looks like?

It wasn't until years into her healing that she realized she spent so much time "doing better" that she hadn't stopped to ask if she was being herself.

Every decision she thought was her own... wasn't.

Amara had been moving through life powered by programming—conditioned responses, generational survival strategies, and masks she picked up to make it through the day.

She didn't even realize the version of her that people loved, respected, and expected… wasn't actually her.

It was the safe version. The palatable one. The one that didn't scare people with too much truth. The one who smiled while grieving, served while empty, and said yes while screaming no.

And when **Amara** finally slowed down, she realized something gut-wrenching: she didn't know how to love anyone unconditionally… because she had never loved herself. Not fully. Not fiercely. Not honestly.

So she grieved. She grieved the little girl who had to lie to survive.

The young woman who thought being a "good person" would guarantee safety.

The adult who confused performance with purpose, and people-pleasing with love.

Amara cried over the roles she mastered and the boundaries she never learned to set.

She mourned the masks that once protected her but now kept her hidden.

It was hard to look in the mirror and not recognize herself.

But what came next was the most radical act she could've chosen:

She decided to stop performing forgiveness and start practicing compassion.

Not the kind that lets you off the hook—but the kind that lets you come home to yourself.

Blueprint Breakdown: Compassion in Action

Compassion isn't about coddling the past. It's about honoring pain without making it your personality.

True compassion says: *"You did what you had to do to survive. And now that you're safe…you can do it differently."*

This kind of grace is layered. It peels back the lies. It forces you to grieve, not just what happened to you—but how you disappeared in order to cope.

Compassion is not passive. It's active grief. It's soul-deep work. And it's the soil where self-love takes root.

Help See Yourself Clearly

- Have you confused being "strong" with self-abandoning?

- What parts of yourself have you never allowed to be seen, even by you?

- Who did you pretend to be in order to be loved—and are you ready to let her rest?

- What would it look like to meet your younger self with compassion instead of shame?

Try This: INNEREVOLUTION in Action

Find a photo of your younger self—the one who was still figuring it all out. Look at her for a full minute. Then say out loud: *"You didn't deserve what happened. You deserved to be loved, to be seen, to be safe."*

If tears come, let them. That's not weakness. That's release.

Anchor It: A Truth to Carry

"I give grace to the girl who did what she had to do—and I honor the woman I've become because of her."

Story: The Common Denominator

Keisha started noticing the pattern in middle school.

It was subtle at first—name-calling on the school bus. "Skeletor."

Too skinny. Too dark. Too… different.

The words didn't just sting. They stuck.

She noticed it again when she saw the birthday party pictures flood the timeline. Everyone was smiling. Everyone was invited. Everyone but her. No explanation. Just silence.

She noticed it at work—again and again—when someone else got the credit, the promotion, the recognition. Even when she was the most qualified. Even when she'd trained the person who got the job.

Keisha noticed it in friendships, in old lovers, in all the places she kept returning to—after being dismissed, betrayed, left out, overlooked

And one day it hit her.

I was there every time.

She wasn't the villain. But she was the common denominator.

Keisha was present in every moment she chose not to choose herself.

Not out of weakness—but out of conditioning.

She learned early that her needs were optional. That care was something you earned by proving you were easy to love. Easy to keep around.

So she became adaptable. Forgiving. Overly understanding.

She extended grace to everyone but herself.

Until one day she didn't.

Until one day she finally said: *"I deserve better than the crumbs of connection."*

That day, care stopped being something **Keisha** gave away to get love—and started being the guide to come home to herself.

Blueprint Breakdown: Care in Action

Real care requires clarity. You can't care for yourself if you don't believe you're worthy.

It's not selfish to prioritize your needs—it's strategic. It's sacred. Care looks like boundaries. Rest. Nourishment. Saying no without a 15-minute explanation. Saying yes to things that actually make your soul breathe. When you've been conditioned to abandon yourself, choosing care will feel like rebellion.

Do it anyway.

Help See Yourself Clearly

- In what moments have you chosen to be included over being respected?

- What does true self-care look like beyond bubble baths and canceling plans?

- Who have you become to be accepted—and what has it cost you?

- Where in your life are you still hoping they'll "see your worth" instead of living it out loud?

Try This: INNEREVOLUTION in Action

Set a 5-minute timer. Write down everything you need in this season to feel cared for— emotionally, physically, spiritually.

Then circle the one thing you've been avoiding or deprioritizing.

That's your starting point.

Make space for it this week. No apologies.

Anchor It: A Truth to Carry

"I am no longer abandoning myself to feel chosen. I choose me—and that's more than enough."

Story: The Climb Never Lied

They say once you know better, you do better. But what they don't say is how frustrating it feels when you know better… and still keep slipping.

Tameka remembered crying to her therapist, exhausted and confused.

"When does it stop feeling like I'm always falling apart?"

The therapist responded with an image—a mountain. Healing, she said, was like climbing. You ascend. You trip. You slide back. But you keep climbing.

At the time, it felt like empty comfort. **Tameka** didn't want metaphors. She wanted peace. What she didn't realize was that the climb *was* peace… in motion.

So she kept going.

Climbing. Crying. Waiting. Starting over.

Again, and again and again.

What changed everything was when she stopped needing to "feel motivated" to stay the course—and started choosing discipline as an act of devotion to her future self. Consistency stopped being about perfection. It became about direction.

Tameka carved out time for herself in a life that once belonged to everyone else.

She started saying no to being the background character in other people's dreams.

She made room for her own.

But it wasn't easy. It never is. Because consistency requires clarity of purpose and compassion for the process.

It demands you decide who you want to become—and keep showing up as her, even when it's hard, lonely, or inconvenient.

That's what **Tameka** learned:

Consistency isn't about never falling. It's about never forgetting who you're becoming.

Blueprint Breakdown: Consistency in Action

Consistency is not sexy. It's not loud. It rarely gets applause. But it's sacred.

It's the daily decision to return to yourself. To your truth. To your vision. Not because it's easy, but because it's yours. You don't need to be perfect to be consistent. You just need to be present.

Present with the patterns. Present with the progress. And present with the version of you who's still learning how to trust the journey.

Help See Yourself Clearly

- What stories have you told yourself about why you "can't stick with it?"

- In what ways have you equated inconsistency with failure, instead of feedback?

- Are your daily habits aligned with your future self—or are they keeping you comfortable in your past?

- What would change if you treated discipline as an act of care, not punishment?

Try This: INNEREVOLUTION in Action

Pick one thing that brings you closer to who you're becoming—just one.

Commit to it for the next 7 days. Keep it simple. Keep it honest.

Track how it feels, not just how it performs.

Anchor It: A Truth to Carry

"Consistency is not about never falling. It's about never forgetting that I am worth getting back up for."

***

If you've made it here, I hope you've realized something important: This isn't a workbook.

This isn't a chapter. This is a mirror.

And you? You're not broken. You're not too far gone. You're not behind. You're not "doing it wrong." You are human. And you are healing.

Curiosity showed you how to ask better questions.

Clarity reminded you that your truth doesn't need to be voted on.

Courage taught you to keep showing up—even when no one claps.

Compassion offered grace for every version of yourself that helped you survive.

Care taught you that your needs are not a burden.

Consistency is the promise you will keep to yourself when it's no longer about proving anything to anybody.

You don't have to wait for permission. You don't need to be more of anything. You only need to be willing. Willing to be seen. To be felt. To be known—first, by you. And you've always been enough.

This is the real   INNEREVOLUTION. And it's just getting started.

Because **YOU** are the blueprint.

Notes

These pages are for you—your reflections, breakthroughs, questions, and reminders.
Write what you need to say. Cross it out. Rewrite it.
This is your space to be messy, honest, and free.

_____

_____

_____

_____

_____

_____

_____

_____

_____

_____

_____

_____

_____

_____

_____

_____

Chapter Nine

Conclusion: The Beginning of Your Radical Journey

You didn't pick up this book by accident. Something deep inside you knew it was time… time to stop waiting. Time to stop searching for the perfect moment. Time to stop over-explaining your needs and start honoring them.

And here you are.

At the end of this book—but at the very beginning of what matters most: Your next chapter. Written for you, by you.

You already know what needs to be done.

You've spent enough time gathering wisdom, analyzing your patterns, and preparing for change. You've now walked through the INNEREVOLUTION—an intimate, unfiltered look at what it actually takes to stop abandoning yourself and start becoming *yourself*.

So the question isn't *if* you can do this.

The question is: **Will you?**

Will you show up for yourself...

Not just when it's easy.

Not just when it's convenient. But when no one is watching.

This is not a gentle pat on the back. This is not a quiet suggestion to maybe take action someday.

This is a call-in to the version of you that's waiting on the other side of consistency, courage, and *self-trust*.

The truth...

You already have everything you need.

The stories you've read, the questions you've answered, the tears you may have shed— they weren't just part of one chapter. They are your *awakening*.

The C6 Blueprint™—Curiosity, Clarity, Courage, Compassion, Care, and Consistency—isn't just a framework.

It's a way of being. It's the guide you'll return to when life gets loud. It's the reminder that growth doesn't always feel graceful. And it's the proof that you don't have to wait until you're healed to start.

You have permission to begin right now—as you are.

- <u>Curiosity</u> will help you ask better questions instead of staying stuck in assumptions.
- <u>Clarity</u> will guide you to honor what actually matters to you.

- Courage will move you, even when fear tries to keep you still.

- Compassion will soften your inner voice and remind you that growth doesn't require perfection.

- Care will ground you in rituals that restore instead of deplete.

- Consistency will help you become the person who doesn't just dream—but builds.

So let me say this, clearly and directly:

You are not broken.

You are not too late. You are not behind.

You are right on time for your own evolution.

Let this be the last time you nod in agreement and do nothing. Let this be the last time you water down your truth to keep the peace. Let this be the last time you let fear, doubt, or perfectionism make you forget who you are.

Take the first step.

A small, intentional, undeniable act that says: *"I choose me."*

Then take another. And another. One decision at a time. This isn't about chasing perfection. It's about coming home to yourself, again and again. It's about doing the work, building trust with your own soul, and finally—finally—believing that you are worthy of your own damn life.

And as you rise, remember this:

This is your time. This is your moment.

Now go make yourself proud.

Notes

These pages are for you—your reflections, breakthroughs, questions, and reminders.
Write what you need to say. Cross it out. Rewrite it.
This is your space to be messy, honest, and free.

Epilogue

Writing this book was never just about putting words on paper—it was about becoming the person I was always meant to be.

And I didn't do it alone.

This journey, like so many others in my life, was shaped by the people who supported, challenged, and stood beside me, even when I wasn't sure I could stand on my own.

Acknowledgments

***

To my Great Uncle Bruce

It was at that old wooden picnic table in the dining room where you looked at me and challenged me to want more for myself among other things, he said, "You should write book, you got a story to tell."

That moment never left me.

Thank you for seeing something in me long before I could see it in myself.

I wish you were here to hold this signed copy in your hands.

But I know you're still with me—every page, every word, every step.

***

To my family

Thank you for holding me accountable—not just in words, but in action. Your unwavering support and the way you push me to be better have been the foundation of my resilience.

***

To my oldest daughter

I continue to look forward to the day I can reintroduce myself to you.

Until then, know this: I love you beyond measure.

No distance, no time, no circumstance will ever change that.

***

To my youngest daughter

By experiencing you, I know that I have done well.

Watching you become your own person fills me with indescribable pride.

Fly, baby. You were always meant to soar.

***

To my sister and brother

Had I not desired to give you both the very best in life, I'm unsure of when I would have discovered resilience, drive, and the motivation to become someone different.

You were my first lesson in responsibility, my first motivation for success, and my constant reminder that love requires action.

Thank you for shaping me, even when you didn't know you were.

Acknowledgments

***

To my friends

The ones who never questioned it, never hesitated, and always supported my extravagant ideas and wild shenanigans—you are the ones who remind me that I am never alone.

You believe in me on the days I doubt myself, and you never ask me to shrink to make anyone else comfortable.

That kind of friendship is rare, and I do not take it for granted.

***

To the people I've met along the way

Leaders, mentors, military co-workers, and friends—you all had a hand in molding me.

Some of you taught me through wisdom and guidance; others taught me through challenge and adversity.

Both were necessary.

***

To My Illustrator

Thank you, Ksenija Petranovic, for taking the vision in my heart and giving it shape, color, and soul.

You didn't just draw—you translated emotion into image.

Every line carries intention, and every detail reflects care.

Your artistry helped me tell the truth in more than just words, and for that, I'm deeply grateful.

***

To My Editor

Thank you Roneshia Thomas for honoring my voice while sharpening my message.

You didn't just clean up my words—you held space for them.

You pushed me when I needed it, clarified what felt muddy, and reminded me that my story mattered.

This book is stronger because of your insight, your honesty, and your unwavering belief in the process.

***

To You—The One Who Reads This Far

Because I got to take my time with this, I want to leave something here just in case you're the only one who reads this far.

You are my favorite.

Having the opportunity to not only learn from you but to love you has been the most rewarding experience of my life.

Acknowledgments

You keep me grounded when I feel unsteady, shielded in ways I didn't know I needed, and safe in ways I never knew I wanted.

You are the calm in my storm, the anchor in my wandering, and the home I never knew I was searching for.

I am in love with you. And I look forward to every adventure we will have together.

Thank you for seeing me.

Thank you for loving me.

And thank you for reading The Art of Saving Your Damn Self™.

About the Author

Kiana Jordan is a self-liberation coach for Black women who've spent their lives being what everyone else needed—strong, silent, accommodating, and exhausted. She helps them unlearn the roles they were conditioned to perform and remember who they were *before* survival became their full-time job.

A retired Air Force Senior NCO turned Culture Coach, Kiana uses her signature *C6 Blueprint*™ to guide women through inner revolutions that feel like coming home. Her work isn't about self-improvement—it's about *self-return*.

Through storytelling, systems of care, and radical honesty, she helps Black women reclaim their time, voice, and truth—so they can live unmasked, untamed, and unapologetically free.

She lives in Fort Walton Beach, Florida, where she writes, rests, reclaims, and reminds women that being yourself is the most powerful thing you can do.

To explore her tools and teachings, visit www.kianajordan.com—where the journey continues beyond the page, into truth, tenderness, and your own liberation.

www.ingramcontent.com/pod-product-compliance
Lightning Source LLC
Chambersburg PA
CBHW020546030426
42337CB00013B/982